AIKIDO

AIKIDO

Bruce Allemann

NEW HOLLAND

First published in 2004 by
New Holland Publishers Ltd
London • Cape Town • Sydney • Auckland
www.newhollandpublishers.com

86 Edgware Road
London W2 2EA
United Kingdom

80 McKenzie Street
Cape Town 8001
South Africa

14 Aquatic Drive
Frenchs Forest, NSW 2086
Australia

218 Lake Road
Northcote, Auckland
New Zealand

ISBN 1 84330 591 7 (paperback)

Publisher: Mariëlle Renssen
Managing Editors: Claudia Dos Santos, Simon Pooley
Studio Manager: Richard MacArthur
Commissioning Editor: Alfred LeMaitre
Editor: Di Kilpert
Designer: Tanja Schulz
Production: Myrna Collins
Consultant: Chris Bartley (4th Dan),
certified coach tutor for the British Aikido Board

Reproduction by Unifoto Pty Ltd
Printed and bound in Malaysia by Times Offset (M) Sdn. Bhd.

2 4 6 8 10 9 7 5 3 1

DISCLAIMER

The author and publishers have made every effort to ensure that the information contained in this book was accurate at the time of going to press, and accept no responsibility for any injury or inconvenience sustained by any person using this book or following the advice provided herein.

CONTENTS

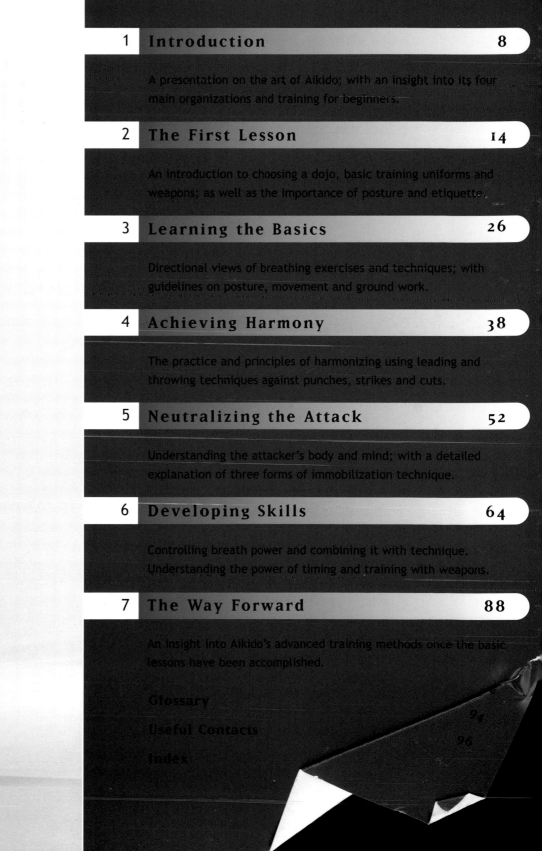

Aikido is the legacy of Morihei Ueshiba (*O Sensei* — the 'Great Teacher'), whose philosophy is the foundation of the art today. In 1925 he reached a turning point in his life when he came to understand the connection between the martial way (*budo*) and the spiritual way. This enlightenment led him to create a new martial art that he believed had the power to unite the world. He called it the Way of Harmony of Life Force — *Aikido*. This is the joy of Aikido: it is both a martial art and an ethical way of life, a physical technique for self-defence and a spiritual self-improvement technique for a happier, healthier world.

The Japanese word *ai* does not translate well into English. *Ai* is often translated as 'love', but it is not the same as the Western concept of love; it also carries connotations of harmony or 'oneness' with nature. *Ki* is the vital life energy — the force that governs the universe and holds it together. *Do* is 'the way to' or 'the way of'. *Ai-ki-do* is therefore 'the way to harmonize with the power of the universe'.

The origins of Aikido

The founder of Aikido, Morihei Ueshiba (1883–1969), developed Aikido through a lifelong process of study and training. The lessons he learned are encapsulated in the Aikido techniques, which are in a sense a short cut to what he learned throughout his life. Many students follow his path, focusing initially on physical and technical development and becoming more metaphysical and philosophical in later life.

As a young man growing up in Tanabe, Japan, Morihei is reported to have been extremely strong despite his small stature. Through rigorous training and self-discipline he developed physical strength and stamina, which were supplemented by his training in martial arts and his military service. He enlisted in the Japanese army in 1903, where he received rapid promotion through his service in the Russo-Japanese War of 1904–05, developing a reputation for unusual prowess with the bayonet and an uncanny ability to sense impending attacks.

By 1912 he had met one of his most influential teachers, Sokaku Takeda, Grand Master of Daitoryu Aiki jiu jitsu. Daitoryu was one of the most respected early schools of unarmed combat, characterized by the fluid use of the body as a weapon. Sokaku was a highly respected man who travelled widely, attracting many disciples through his talent and technique. Morihei was

...hiba

so impressed by him that he built a *dojo* (training hall) with a shrine to the master on his property in Hokkaido so that Sokaku could live there and teach him. He studied with Master Sokaku until his return to his birthplace, Tanabe, in 1919, by which time he had become an unusually proficient swordsman and Aiki jiu jitsu proponent. At the age of 30 he began studying with Master Deguchi Onisaburo, the leader of the Omote Kyu religious sect, and for the next 13 years he travelled with Onisaburo through China, Manchuria and Korea, returning to Japan in 1924.

By this time his pursuit of *budo* had matured into the principled art that he called Aikido. He spent the rest of his life teaching it to a succession of disciples and students from all over the world and from all walks of life: scholars, policemen, soldiers, other martial arts experts and even actors and dancers. Men, women and children studied with him, and the art flourished with the aid of senior students such as Saito Sensei, Tohei Sensei, Yamada Sensei and Yamaguchi Sensei. In 1968 Morihei was hospitalized with liver cancer. He refused surgery and returned home, continuing to teach until his death on 26 April 1969.

What can Aikido do for me?

Newcomers have varying ideas about what Aikido can do for them: self-development, gaining self-confidence, healthy exercise, intellectual stimulation, meeting people, competing, controlling their aggression or finding spiritual enlightenment.

Many novices, particularly women, want to learn self-defence. They do not want to be the victims of crime and violence. Aikido can help them live their lives with confidence and joy.

I'KKYO - BASIC ARM CONTROL IS ONE OF SEVERAL FUNDAMENTAL TECHNIQUES OF AIKIDO.

Some newcomers start training because they want to be respected for their fighting prowess, in the Hollywood mould. Many of these lose interest when they realize that to reach the levels they dream of takes time, hard work and self-discipline. Those who stay discover that learning respect for self and for others matters more than seeking personal glory, especially in conflict situations. Aikido teaches you to be neither aggressor nor victim nor escalator of violence. This is not just a philosophical or ethical teaching: harmony is encouraged because it is more effective than aggression. It creates strong individuals who live without fear or hatred.

Some of those who come to Aikido for academic or esoteric reasons give up when they realize that the training entails being thrown to the ground, having their joints manipulated and being attacked. But it is through Aikido's physical training that those who stick it out find what they are looking for. Hidden inside the exercises, forms and techniques are deeper meanings that emerge whether you are looking for them or not.

People who practise Aikido report improved health, lower levels of stress, greater self-confidence and enhanced social skills, such as better relationships with their colleagues or superiors. If you are prepared to put in some hard work you will find what you are looking for, although often not in the way you expected.

Basic principles

Aikido is primarily a grappling rather than striking martial art. It uses elegant flowing circular moves, entering and pivoting to control and disperse an attack. Anticipation, timing, a stable and flexible posture and well-balanced body movements enable you to destabilize the assailant and enlist their power in your own defence. The force is provided by the attacker.

Coordinated movements, relaxed breathing and well-timed transfer of body weight are used in throwing and pinning techniques. These principles enable you to defend yourself against larger or stronger assailants. Because it does not depend on great physical strength, Aikido is suitable for both sexes and all age groups.

The Aikido philosophy is to use minimal force. However, owing to the rotation and locking techniques, a very small movement may have a dramatic effect on the aggressor. More skilled *aikidoka* will deal with minor encounters by means of avoidance or deflection techniques, reserving the potentially dangerous techniques for life-threatening situations. If violence can be defused without the attacker losing face then this should be attempted, as the outcome is not only sensible from a self-defence point of view, but will also keep both parties on the right side of the law.

But Aikido is not just about self-defence. It is also fun, and good exercise for body, mind and spirit. It is great for improving coordination and balance, especially as you lose your fear of falling. Once you become an experienced *uke* the fun really starts.

Beginning to train

As a beginner you are encouraged to train slowly so you can identify problems and correct them as they occur. At first even simple stepping and turning can be confusing. You practise the basic footwork and learn to fall and roll safely. After a few months you will be familiar with movements like *irimi, tenkan* and *tsugiashi* and will be ready to learn new techniques. Once the basic footwork has become second nature you can watch a technique being demonstrated and immediately begin to imitate its moves. (The subtle hand positions and other refinements come later.) Until you reach this stage you are, of course, really only learning in the *mind*: it takes repetition for the body to learn and the moves to become second nature. Once the body begins to react instinctively, allowing you to concentrate on improving your skills, you can quickly get started with the basic shape and timing of a new attack.

Paying creative attention

When watching a technique for the first time you should not try to analyse it too much. Instead, create a moving picture in your mind, starting with the basic shape and direction of the movements and filling in more detail with each repetition. In times gone by, samurai would pay exorbitant fees to be shown a single technique by

UDEKEMINAGE - LOCKING THE ARM FOR A THROW

an expert. One viewing had to be enough to learn the technique for themselves. Both beginners and advanced students need to develop this ability so as to benefit from top instructors when they are available and make the most of limited training time.

Making progress

The *kyu* (student grade) syllabus usually starts at 6th or 5th *kyu* and works up to 1st *kyu* and then to *shodan* (1st *dan*), which entitles the student to wear a black belt. The highest rank ever awarded by O Sensei was *judan* (10th dan). *Kyu* grading in Aikido is based on formal tests of attacks and defences, with the student alternating between the roles of *uke* and *tori*.

Beginners are tested on basic exercises, techniques and rolls. For the more advanced *kyu* grades, the number and complexity of techniques increases and the standard of smoothness and control which must be achieved is higher. The techniques from the lower *kyu* grades form the basis of all subsequent training. These can be practised at an advanced level by an experienced person while partnering a junior person who is still learning the basics.

Aikido today

After the death of the founder of Aikido, senior teachers broke away to form their own organizations, which today are represented by four main groups.

Aikikai (The *Aiki* Association)

This is the traditional Aikido organization in Japan. The international Aikikai, established officially on 9 February 1948, was the first international Aikido organization. The founder of Aikido, O Sensei Morihei Ueshiba, was its first head. After his death his son, Kisshomaru Ueshiba (1921–99), later followed by his grandson Moriteru Ueshiba, was invested with the hereditary title of *Doshu*, 'Master of the Way', and acted as titular head of the organization and official representative of Hombu Dojo (headquarters) in Japan. Hombu Dojo retains control of technical matters for the organization, although the International Aikido Federation is the chief administrative body. All *dan* gradings are still ratified by Hombu Dojo, although there are many authorized instructors who perform the actual grading tests around the world. The International Aikikai is made up of hundreds of separate organizations that still subscribe to the traditional authority of Hombu Dojo in Tokyo.

The *Ki* Society

One of O Sensei's most senior and respected students, Koheichi Tohei Sensei, formed the Ki Society after O Sensei's death. The Ki Society emphasized the training of *ki*, making it possible to study *ki* without actually studying Aikido. Classes in the Ki Society usually start with a session of pure *ki* training, followed by a session of Aikido. Popular both in Japan and in the West, Ki Society Aikido has a large following and there are many affiliated Ki Society organizations around the world.

The International Yoshinkan Aikido Federation

Gozo Shioda Sensei, who was a student of Morihei Ueshiba for about 8 years, was the founder of Yoshinkan Aikido, which has spread throughout the world, although its spiritual roots remain in Tokyo, Japan. Shioda's enthusiasm for Aikido and his close association with the Tokyo Metropolitan Police have influenced the popularity of his organization and fostered respect for his teachings. Because it is geared to practical applications, Yoshinkan Aikido focuses on a smaller subset of core techniques which Shioda Sensei identified as most useful and reliable.

Tomiki Sport Aikido

Tomiki Sensei, who studied for a long time with the founder of judo, Jigoro Kano, before moving on to Aikido with Morihei Ueshiba, formulated his own style of sport Aikido in the late 1940s. Impatient with Morihei's classical approach, which discourages the sporting and competitive aspects of Aikido training, Tomiki developed a system that includes sparring and competition. Tomiki sport Aikido is taught extensively in schools and universities in Japan and has grown in popularity internationally.

THE FIRST LESSON

The first lesson in Aikido contains everything you need to know. It is about Aikido *form*. Learning the form is a simple task which, paradoxically, takes most of us a lifetime. We know that the techniques of Aikido are the way to learn the form, but it is not so easy to grasp what the form *is*. Perhaps this is just as well, for the delight of studying a form is that the more we understand it, the more there is to understand. The more we unravel the principles, the deeper they become and the more amazed we are at their power and mystery. The joy of Aikido lies in the subtleties we encounter as our skill develops, and our ultimate goal is to *live* the teachings of the first lesson.

The *dojo*

The training hall for a Japanese martial art is called a *dojo*. A traditional Aikido *dojo* is a small building or room with a wooden floor. The floor is covered — often from wall to wall — by a mat called a *tatami*, leaving only a small uncovered section near the entrance where you remove your footwear. Japanese *tatami* are made of individual blocks about one metre wide by two metres long, firm enough to provide a solid surface to move on and to prevent injury when you fall. The best ones are handmade out of tightly packed straw covered with canvas, like those which are used as floor covering in traditional Japanese homes.

At one side of the *dojo*, usually away from the entrance, is a formal focus point, the *kamiza*, or 'upper seat'. This may consist of a scroll featuring Japanese *kanji* calligraphy, a picture of an influential teacher, a picture of O Sensei, or a combination of all three. The *kamiza* may also include a small platform with a bowl of rice or a vase containing a blossoming branch.

Financial constraints may oblige your *dojo* to rent space from a sports centre or local community hall, where the *tatami* and *kamiza* have to be installed for each class and removed afterwards. The *tatami* may be ordinary judo or gymnastics mats covered with a tarpaulin. Whatever the case, the *dojo* is a special place and the venue and the equipment should be respected and carefully looked after.

Choosing a *dojo*

Depending on where you live and what time you have available to you, you may not have much choice. However, it is wise to do some homework about a potential *dojo*, its students and the teacher, *(sensei)*. Try to find out what organization the *dojo* is affiliated to and select one that suits your interests and requirements. Ask to see the instructor's credentials and if possible check them out with an official body. To be good, your instructor need not be associated with the larger Aikido organizations, but you should be cautious of one who is not recognized at all outside his or her own *dojo*. In general, an instructor who has references from recognized masters is a safer bet. Because you will be accepting the teacher as a guide and a role model it is important that his or her character and ethics are similar to your own. It is difficult to learn from someone you do not respect or whose value system is very different from yours. Rather than learn inferior technique or lose your commitment, take time to seek an alternative, even if less convenient, *dojo*. Keep an open mind, accepting that at this stage you will not know exactly what you are looking for, but trust your instincts if the teacher refuses to provide credentials or has a strange attitude.

opposite: ROLLING WHEN THROWN

What will I need to start training?

Clothing

The *keiko gi* is the basic training uniform. It is the same as a judo or jiu jitsu suit. A karate *gi* is generally not strong enough to survive a grappling martial art such as Aikido. The Aikido *gi* consists of a white, double-stitched jacket, and trousers with extra padding at the knees to extend its life. In most Aikido schools students wear white belts to hold the jacket closed, while *dan* graded members wear a black belt, which indicates the end of student grades and is universally associated with Japanese martial arts achievement. (In Aikido, however, it is important to see this achievement as really just the beginning of the student's true understanding of the art.) Teachers and senior students also wear the traditional *hakama* - black or indigo ankle-length skirt-like pleated trousers, common to other Japanese martial arts, especially weapons arts such as *kendo* (the art of sword fighting) and *iado* (the art of drawing the sword). In several Aikido organizations beginners also wear *hakama* and some use a coloured belt system to recognize student grades, as is common practice in judo and karate.

HAKAMA

Weapons for training

Some Aikido schools may not train with weapons, so you should check before you buy anything. Aikido traditionally uses three main weapons: knife, sword and wooden staff. In practice, the four-foot staff or *jo* we train with is the real thing, but for the knife and sword we use replicas: the wooden knife (*tanto*) and the wooden training sword (*bokken*), which replaces the magnificent *katana* sword that was wielded by the samurai of feudal Japan.

THE TRAINING UNIFORM

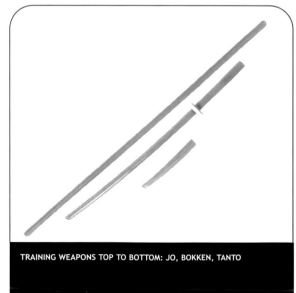

TRAINING WEAPONS TOP TO BOTTOM: JO, BOKKEN, TANTO

The etiquette of Aikido

As Aikido is a Japanese martial art, the etiquette on the *tatami* has a Japanese flavour. Although westerners may feel uncomfortable with some of the formalities in the *dojo*, it is important to understand some basic Japanese social niceties. These are not just decoration, but are closely bound up with the principles and philosophy of Aikido.

For the Japanese, the formal greeting and way to show respect is to bow (*rei*) forward from the waist. This can be done from a standing or sitting position.

The standing bow (*tachirei*)

⇨ Stand with hands to the sides or on your thighs and bend forward from the waist. Avoid direct eye contact, while maintaining awareness of the other person all the time.

The sitting bow (*zarei*)

↘ This is done from *seiza* (the traditional sitting position in Japan), which may prove uncomfortable for many students to start with. In *seiza* the student sits flat on his feet, with the toes touching lightly at the back and knees spread very slightly to the sides. The back is straight and the body relaxed and balanced over the midpoint between the knees and the feet. The hands lie loosely, palms down on the knees and facing slightly inwards.

↘ For the sitting bow (*zarei*), the left hand is placed on the mat, followed by the right hand, to form a triangle of the space between the hands. (*See* p18.)

⇩ The back is kept straight as the head is brought forward and down into the *rei*. The weight is kept on the triangle formed by the feet and knees and the hands are not used for support but merely to project energy. This is an important position to practice as most Aikido ground work is performed on the knees and the *zarei* position is used in several of the arm-lock pins. (A pin is achieved by applying pressure against a joint, trapping the body against the ground or another fixed object.)

↘ The *zarei* may also be performed from *keiza*, which is an alternative sitting position in which the heels are raised so that you balance on your toes. *Keiza* is a more mobile position because it is easier to move and to stand up when the toes are carrying some of the weight. (See the section on *shikko* – p36.)

The bow signifies respect for Aikido, for the teachings of O Sensei, for your teacher and for your fellow students. It is freely and unconditionally given when training in Aikido. Mutual respect is essential for true learning to take place. If students and teachers do not show proper respect for one another and the art then they would be more suited to some other form of training and should move on. Aikido schools may differ in terms of specific formalities in the *dojo*, but without these basic good manners the spirit of Aikido will not be present. Common courtesies such as arriving on time, waiting at the side of the mat to be invited onto it if you are late, accepting the teacher's instructions and not speaking while instruction is being given are all part of this spirit.

A formal bow (*rei*) is made in the direction of the *kamiza*

■ when entering or leaving the *dojo*
■ at the beginning and end of the class
■ when entering or leaving the mat space

The *rei* is also used

■ to indicate your intention to train with someone
■ to thank somebody for training with you
■ to indicate the need to consult with someone

Before training, students should remove any hard or sharp objects such as watches or jewellery, and keep their nails short and their hair tied up if it is long. Personal hygiene is important as no one likes to train with someone who is wearing a smelly *gi* or has not brushed their teeth. *Aikidoka* (Aikido practitioners) should not arrive at training drunk or in any state that could be a danger to themselves or others. Maintaining the appropriate respect for each other promotes safety in the *dojo* and ensures that everyone on the Aikido mat enjoys the training.

In our *dojo* we start and end the class with a formal *zarei*. At the beginning we say 'Onogaeshi imasu', which means 'Please teach me'. Because Aikido is learned through practice with training partners, we all learn from one another. During the class, students are encouraged not to talk to one another, but to use the bow to communicate. In the final *zarei*, we thank each other in Japanese, saying 'Domo arigato gozaimasu' – 'Thank you very much'. During instruction students sit in the *seiza* position and watch the teacher's demonstration as closely as possible. After this they pair off to train. More experienced *aikidoka* train together with beginners and adjust their speed and force to their partner's level of ability. This is common practice in many Aikido schools throughout the world. The experienced students help the beginners, and they in turn help the experienced by reacting in unorthodox ways to the techniques, providing an excellent test of ability and control.

Form versus technique

The words 'form' and 'technique' have specialized meanings in Aikido. Form is the essence of the art. It is what remains when the techniques are stripped away and you find yourself dealing with a unique situation for which a specific technique has not yet been devised. Techniques are the tools that are used to study and develop good form. On their own they may work in many situations, but the best form is free style – unrestricted, unpremeditated and creative. Form is an understanding of the nature of the universe. It cannot be grasped by the mind alone. It is developed by practising the techniques of Aikido with other like-minded individuals until it begins to shape not only your physical practice but also the way you live your life. Your own personality and experiences will influence and direct the form, as will your teachers, fellow students and the training itself. This is why O Sensei called the art Aikido instead of Aiki jiu jitsu. Jiu jitsu is a fighting method, whereas *do* means 'a way of life'. Aikido is the martial way to harmonize with the life force. So how do you begin?

In the first few lessons you will be taught the basics of Aikido form – how to stand, how to move, and how to roll. You may be taught a few actual Aikido techniques but these are not as important as the basic forms. Many martial arts share common techniques, but what differentiates them is the form in which the techniques are realized.

Training in pairs

Because the techniques are performed with a partner, Aikido is extremely difficult, if not impossible, to study on your own. Much of the early training will be *kihonwaza* (basic practice). There are 50 to 60 *kata* (set forms, or patterns of movement), where both *tori* (the person who executes the technique) and *uke* (the person who attacks and then receives the technique) have very specific roles to play. In the *dojo* you will be introduced to the basic techniques and their many variations and applications.

In many Aikido schools competition is considered counterproductive, and in traditional Aikido it is actively discouraged. More experienced *aikidoka* are exposed to advanced training such as *kaeshiwaza* (countertechniques), *jiyuwaza* (free technique against specified attacks), and *rondoriwaza* (free training).

In *rondoriwaza*, *uke* is free to choose any form of attack and *tori* may use any Aikido defence. This is the closest many *aikidoka* come to sparring. In the various Aikido schools there are significant differences of emphasis, especially in the more advanced forms of training. In *Tomiki* sport Aikido a form of competition has been introduced, but the more traditional schools do not follow this practice.

The importance of *hanmi* (posture)

In Aikido training the body is held in a balanced and relaxed upright position throughout the technique. The feet are positioned one behind the other in a straight line pointing in the direction of the attack, with the front foot turned slightly to the side, and the back foot at an angle of 90 degrees to the front one. Bend the front knee and straighten the back leg so that the weight is just behind the front foot. It may feel strange to keep the feet in this position, especially with the weight forward, but with practice you will soon feel comfortable and able to move around freely in this posture. Stay as relaxed as you would be when walking normally. Keep the feet no more than shoulder width apart, the shoulders relaxed and the back straight. Project slightly upwards through the top of the head and project the hips forward.

Migihanmi (right posture)

⇨ Start with the heels touching, positioned at about 90 degrees to each other.

↘ Shift the hips forward, allowing your hips and shoulders to rotate 30 degrees to the left, and place the right foot in front of the left foot, bending the right knee so that the weight is now positioned slightly behind the right heel. As you move into position, raise the hands upward in an arc. Because of the hip rotation the right shoulder will be further forward.

The right hand may now be raised to eye level, while the left hand is in the same line but further back and raised to chest height.

1

2

Hidarihanmi (left posture)

Hidarihanmi (left posture) is the same as *migihanmi* but is done with the left foot and hand in front. In paired technique, the posture (left or right) is usually described from the perspective of *tori* who is receiving the attack. *Uke*'s feet are described in relation to *tori*. In *gyakuhanmi* (opposite posture), *uke* will therefore have the opposite foot forward. For example, if *tori* is in *hidarihanmi* (left posture), *uke* will be in *migihanmi* (with right side forward). When both *uke* and *tori* have the same side forward this is called *aihanmi* (harmonious posture).

Tori and *uke*

Training in Aikido is almost exclusively performed with a partner. Only during basic warm-up do you train by yourself. Half of the time you will be taking the role of *tori*, the partner applying the Aikido technique against an attack. Often this is what people visualize themselves doing when they start training, so it can come as

a shock to realize that the other half of the time you will have to take the role of *uke*, which is arguably the more important role to master, and the more difficult, especially in the early stages of training. This is a dual role: *uke* is initially the attacker and then, as the technique is applied, the receiver of the technique, and because *tori* uses the force of the attack to perform the technique, it is important to make the correct kind of attack. Beginners often do not know how to do this, or are afraid of getting hurt. They may hold back from attacking or lock up against the technique. This is not good Aikido. As the receiver, it is important to accept, not resist, the technique. It is common for students to resist it to prove they are stronger or that *tori* cannot throw them. This is very easy to do when you are faced with a less experienced *tori* and you know exactly what technique is going to be attempted.

The art of *ukemi* (receiving technique)

The skill of providing the appropriate attack and then receiving the technique, while at the same time protecting yourself from injury, is called *ukemi*. Fear is a common cause of beginner injuries, so it is important to learn right away how to roll when thrown, protect yourself when the joints are locked and control the body safely when off balance. *Ukemi* is an active process. *Uke* should keep control even when off-balance, falling from a projection or reacting to a joint lock. The following are some ways to do this:

■ When a joint lock is applied, relax and accept the lock. When you are unbalanced backwards, use your hips to keep your legs underneath you so you can roll to protect yourself from falling. This is the backward roll (*ushiro ukemi*).
■ If you're taken off-balance towards the front, you may be able to roll forwards over the shoulder (*mai ukemi*).
■ *Tori* may be locking one of the arm joints, preventing a forward roll and forcing *uke* face down onto the mat. In this form push forward on the free arm to convert the fall into a forward slide.

When you are training *kihonwaza (basic practice)*, remember that you are practising set forms or *kata*. Do not resist the technique. Concentrate on protecting yourself by using your own good technique — not on disrupting the *tori*'s technique. On the other hand you are doing the *tori* no favours by attacking poorly. Attacks must be properly directed with appropriate speed and force for your partner's level of ability. Do not fall before the technique is applied, or stop and lock up like a statue after the initial movement. Strive to return to your feet as soon as possible. Do not lie on the ground waiting for the pin or your *tori* will not learn how to keep control to the end of the technique. *Tori* should maintain control continuously — even between one technique and another. This continuous awareness and control between *uke* and *tori* is called *zanshin*.

A final word on *ukemi*. In general *uke* must work harder than *tori* and it is through *ukemi* that you will get fit and gain confidence in your Aikido. There is great satisfaction in knowing that no matter what technique is applied you will always be able to protect yourself and come bouncing back for more.

Practice for Basic *Ukemi* (protection)
Form 1 — *Ushiro ukemi undo* — rolling exercise

↗ Place your left foot behind your right. Bend your knees and roll backwards as if sitting down.

↘ Start in *migihanmi* (right posture).

↗ Roll onto your back, keeping it rounded and your head off the ground.

↘ Roll forward again to a sitting position, switching feet as you roll. Tuck your toes underneath before attempting to stand.

⇐ Rise until you are back on your feet in *gyakuhanmi* (left posture). (Repeat on the other side.)

Form 2 — *Ushiro ukemi* — backward roll

↶ Repeat the first three steps
of the rolling exercise. (Form 1)

↷ Keep your chin tucked
in and tilt your head to
the left-hand side.

⇓ As you roll back-
wards, continue rolling
over your right shoulder.

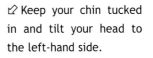

⇨ Return to a standing
position in *migihanmi*.
(Switch legs to repeat
on the other side.)

Form 3 — *Mai ukemi* when pinned

2 ⇩ As your shoulder is pushed into the ground, push your left forearm into the mat above and in front of your head and slide forward to break your fall.

⇧ When your right arm is being locked it may be unsafe to try and roll out of the technique. Keep your arm extended without tension (point through your fingers to keep the correct form) and turn your hips counterclockwise to relieve the pressure on your shoulder joint.

⇨ Turn your head to the left and lift your left knee slightly up to the left side to free your ribs and ease your breathing. Keep extending down through your arm to test for a possible escape route.

Form 4 — *Yoku ukemi* — side protection

↗ Start from *migihanmi*. Bending your right knee, place your left foot in front of your right foot.

⇩ Sit down backwards towards your left side, rolling down the outside of your left leg.

⇩ Slap the mat with the your left forearm and the palm of your left hand to break your fall. (Practise on both sides.)

Form 5 — *Mai ukemi* — forward protection

⇦ From *migihanmi*, bend your knees and lower your slightly curved arms down inside the right knee, rotating the wrists palm down. Turn your hands inwards to point your little fingers towards one another.

⇦ Place your palms on the mat and tumble forward over your right shoulder, rolling on your right arm.

⇗ Keep your back well rounded and your chin tucked down into your chest near your left shoulder.

⇨ Straighten your left leg to bring yourself back up again to a standing position in *migihanmi*. (Repeat on the other side.)

⇩ ⇘ Tuck your left knee in behind your right knee and allow the tumble to carry you over your left leg.

LEARNING THE BASICS

In your first lesson, you are taught how to stand, how to move and how to work with a partner without clashing. You are shown how to roll rather than fall when receiving technique. These exercises, which have been handed on from teacher to teacher, contain in them the essence of the art of Aikido. They focus on relaxed breathing, controlled body movement and protection from injury. To a beginner they look extremely simple and indeed they are. Yet many people find it difficult to reproduce these movements to start off with. Challenges are encountered in even the simplest of exercises or techniques, and as your skill develops you are challenged further. There is always more to discover, no matter how experienced you become. Even the masters of Aikido continually strive towards full understanding.

Kokyuryoku — breath power

All Aikido exercises are based on breath control and breath power. The following are some that are used in many *dojos*.

Basic breathing

Stand up straight with feet to the sides about shoulder width apart. The knees should be slightly bent, while the hands hang down naturally at the sides. Try not to pull the shoulders back but concentrate on a feeling of relaxed balance running from firmly planted feet up the spine and through the top of the head. Allow your body weight to settle down into the soles of your feet where you feel the contact with the mat. Pushing from right down in the gut, empty your lungs through a partly open mouth. Resist the urge to breathe in and keep pushing until all the stale air is expelled. At the end of the out-breath, simply stop pushing and allow the pressure that has built up to draw fresh air in through the nose and start filling the lungs with air. Allow a steady stream of air to enter through your nose at a comfortable rate by expanding your chest and raising your hands palm up until they are above shoulder height and the lungs reach full capacity. Once again, use the chest muscles to hold the air in for a moment as you rotate your palms downwards. When you relax the chest muscles again, this starts pushing the stale air out of the lungs, and the next push from the belly re-empties the lungs while you bring your hands palm down to the sides again, ready for the next cycle.

The in-breath should take slightly longer than the out-breath. A count of 10 on the in-breath, two to hold for a moment, eight to breathe out and two to pause for the next cycle works well. How fast you count will depend on your lung capacity, level of fitness and recent exertion. Although the goal is to slow your breathing down and to take fewer but deeper breaths, you should not feel uncomfortable. Breathe at your own pace and practise daily to develop your control.

The following exercise is good for general stress release and relaxation, and can also be done without the arm movements from a sitting position in your office or in rush hour traffic.

opposite: NIKKYO WRIST LOCK VARIATION

Basic breathing exercise

⇨ Relax, bend slightly at the knees and breathe out.

↘ Breathe in as you let your arms rise palms up to above shoulder height.

⇩ ↘ Now rotate your palms down and allow the pressure from your abdomen to clear your lungs as you return to the first position. (Repeat the cycle several times.)

↘ Maintain the in-breath for two counts after your lungs have filled.

Funetori undo — rowing exercise with breath power

Traditionally, the first Aikido class of the day begins with the rowing exercise, based on the Japanese technique for rowing boats from a standing position using heavy wooden oars. This is an excellent exercise, as it practises full breath power and extension from the centre as in many sitting meditation practices such as *zazen* (from Zen Buddhism), and combines this with a vigorous body action. It helps train the body, mind and spirit to work together harmoniously to keep calm and focused in the heat of combat.

To start, take half a step forward with the left foot pointing forward and the right foot about one-and-a-half foot lengths behind it and at an angle of 90 degrees to the front foot. The hips and shoulders should face squarely to the front and the arms hang down at the sides. Begin the movement by exhaling as the weight of the hips and upper body is transferred backwards towards the back foot. Draw the hands up the sides with palms facing downwards to about navel height.

Now, inhaling the word 'HI', drive the hips forward, extending the hands as if pushing a huge obstacle out of the way. As the lungs reach capacity and the weight settles onto the front foot, the weight is drawn back onto the back foot while you exhale the word 'SU'. The exercise is repeated several times, following which breathing is returned to normal while the hands are clasped and gently shaken. The cycle is repeated on the opposite side with the right foot forward. To accompany the breathing on the right side the words 'HI' and 'SUM' are *kiai*'ed in the same way.

1 Start with the weight well back and the lungs full.
2 Push forward with the hips and project through the arms as you exhale with *kiai*.
3 Draw the hips backwards pushing down with hands.

Kiai is an audible, energetic expression of the spirit of the practitioner. Although many people, especially Western women, are shy about using *kiai*, combined with the rowing exercise it builds confidence and a positive spirit. '*Kiai*' is derived from the same root as '*aiki*'. Literally, the meaning of *ki-ai* is 'breath unification' or 'spirit harmonization'. Good *kiai* resonates from deep within the body's 'one point' (a point 4 cm (1.5in) below the navel) with a powerful piercing sound that can be quite startling to an attacker.

Suwariwaza kokyudoza

It is common practice in many Aikido *dojos* to finish the final lesson of the day with 'sitting breath-power exercises'. Two partners sitting in *seiza* position facing one another at a comfortable touching distance perform this together. In its simple form, *tori* raises the hands slightly towards *uke*. *Tori*'s hands are about shoulder width apart, with the palms facing towards each other and the fingers pointing towards *uke*'s throat. *Uke* initiates the practice by gripping both *tori*'s wrists with 50 per cent power (and pushing and pulling them, to test *tori*'s balance.

Using only the relaxed power of *ki* from the 'one point', *tori* rotates the wrists as if turning a doorknob, causing *uke*'s gripping hands to rotate underneath *tori*'s

wrists. At the same time *tori* breathes in and begins to push in underneath *uke*'s forearms. To maintain a strong grip, *uke* must raise the elbows, shoulders and body (sometimes even being forced to stand.) When *tori* can feel that *uke* is well off-balance and at least partly dependent on *tori* for support, the hands cut away as *tori* exhales and allows *uke* to fall and roll.

Rather than pushing *uke* over with brute strength, *tori* must try to relax and use the force of *uke*'s grip to unbalance *uke*. There will always be somebody stronger. The day when a strong man or woman is weakened by illness or old age should not be the day when his or her Aikido falls to pieces. Practice should be vigorous and powerful but not too forceful.

↙ Start from *seiza* position with *uke* grasping *tori* by the wrists and attempting to trap *tori*'s arms and body. Turn both palms upwards pushing gently into the grip to find *uke*'s power.

⇨ Rotate the palms towards each other and extend with *tegatana* ('hand blade' — the edge of the hand used like a blade).

⬇ Pin *uke* sitting with the weight on the triangle formed by the knees and feet in the *keiza* position. *Uke* must maintain the grip on the wrists and cover the groin for protection.

↘ Turn to the weaker side and break *uke*'s balance.

Posture and dynamic movement

The basic ready position or *kamae* of Aikido is used to receive the force of an attack in a controlled, safe and flexible manner. The *kamae* is not a rigid posture from which to launch a powerful counterattack; it is an ever-changing, fluid state of relaxed power, an expression of the harmony of *ki* energy, which is the central meaning of Aikido. It is not so much a position as a state of mind, body and spirit that can change shape and focus as the circumstances dictate.

To understand posture properly you should train with *uke* of various physiques and abilities. The following basic body movements or *taisabaki* are extremely simple and yet it is mastery of them that will determine your progress. They consist of posture practice, entry steps, turning and groundwork.

Upper body exercises
Ikkyo undo

This exercise trains *tori* in how to raise the hands to defend against a blow to the head.

Step forward with the right leg into right posture. Let the hips flow forward as for the rowing exercise. Both arms swing forward and upward in an arc from below, deflecting an incoming blow upwards and backwards without trying to stop its force. Keep the shoulders down and allow the arms to swing in the shoulder joint without tightening the shoulder muscles. The elbows are slightly bent and the arm muscles are firm but not tight. Use 'unbendable arm' — a relaxed, heavy but extended state that is common in most Aikido techniques. The body weight is kept low and the breath is drawn in as the arms rise. At the top of the arc the body weight is well forward behind the front leg.

As *tori* starts to breathe out, the weight is pushed back onto the back foot as the 'unbendable' arms cut down in an arc back to either side of the body below the hips. The exercise is repeated several times in left posture before swapping to practise again in right posture. While doing the exercise in class, the instructor may want to test your posture by pushing or pulling against your arms, hips and shoulders. Stay relaxed, keeping your weight low. If you do not push

to counteract the tests, your balance and control will develop more rapidly.

1 Start with the weight slightly back, the hands in low position and your lungs full.

2 Cut up with both arms swinging from the shoulders in an arc as you breathe out with a silent *kiai*.

Basic entry
Enter when pulled

The *ikkyo undo* exercise gives you some basic practice in dealing with an incoming attack. To use the force of an attack, *tori* must adapt to variations in height and direction. By varying the height of your defence relative to the attack you will soon begin to deal better with high and low attacks. The direction of the attack will affect your body motion. In general you will turn your hips to accommodate any lateral movement by the attacker.

This may mean changing posture completely, by swapping feet, or simply by pivoting the feet and hips. Another variation of direction an attacker may use is a drawing attack, such as a pull or a grip. This should not be resisted; rather, go with the pull and even exaggerate the motion. The various entry techniques should be practised as often as possible, the two main ones being *tsugiashi* (glide step), and *irimiashi* (entry step).

Tsugiashi — glide step from front foot

Step forward with a gliding motion, with the front foot being followed by the back foot. From right posture with the feet close together (less than one foot-length apart) the hips surge forward along the line of attack as if you plan to step *irimiashi*, but instead the front foot moves forward and to the right. The left leg is drawn in behind the right, off the imaginary line of attack. The final stage is right posture, exactly as you started out.

⇨ Start in *migihanmi* (right posture) with feet close together.

⇨ Project your weight forward by moving the hips and the front foot forward.

⇨ Try to draw the back leg along with the movement of the hips so that the whole movement becomes a single action.

Irimiashi — entry step

This is the exercise of stepping forward from left posture to right posture during an attack. Start from left posture with left foot forward and left hand at chest height. Step forward and slightly to the right with the right foot and then turn the left foot to the left, pulling it off the imaginary line of *uke*'s attack. The hips, which start off facing to the right, finish off facing to the left, with the right hand forward in right posture.

↘ Start in *hidarihanmi* (left posture). Draw the weight forward by bringing the right foot in behind the left.

↗ Turn the hips to the left and step into *migihanmi* (right posture). Your body weight must be transferred to a point just behind the right foot.

Turn when pushed

When the force of the attack is incoming, especially if it is powerful and fast, it is often easier to turn and allow the attack to go past. This is used particularly against pushing, punching, kicking or charging attacks. The basic rule is to turn when pushed and enter when pulled. (You will also need to learn to turn when pulled and enter when pushed, but as a beginner it is best to go with the attack to avoid clashing against the force.) Two useful exercises to practise turning with an attack are *kaiten undo* (a hip-and-foot rotation) and *tenkan undo* (a hip turn-and-step combined).

Kaiten — turning

Kaiten is any hip turn performed without stepping. For example, from right posture, start by turning the head and the hips counterclockwise towards the rear, then swivel round turning on the balls of the feet so that you turn to face the rear in left posture. Shift your body weight from behind the right foot in right posture to behind the left foot in left posture.

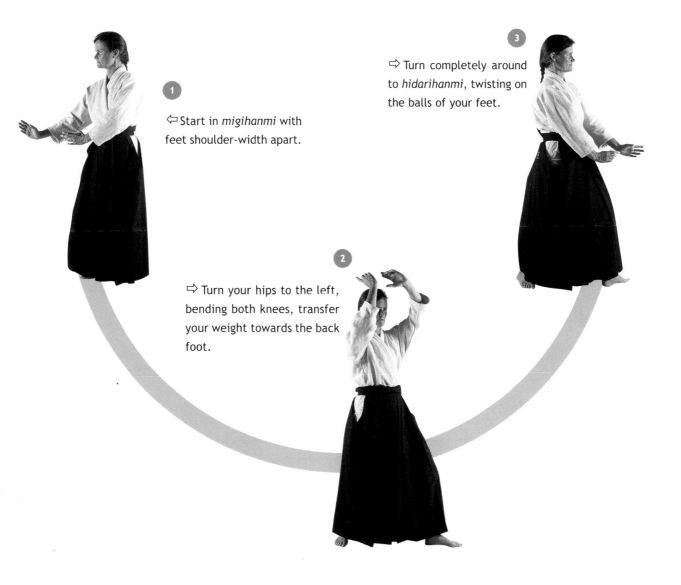

1 ⇐ Start in *migihanmi* with feet shoulder-width apart.

2 ⇨ Turn your hips to the left, bending both knees, transfer your weight towards the back foot.

3 ⇨ Turn completely around to *hidarihanmi*, twisting on the balls of your feet.

Tenkan - backward turning step

From right posture turn to the rear and step backwards. The weight pivots around the front foot while the rear of the body swings around like a door opening. Start with the weight behind the right foot in right posture. Turn counterclockwise as for *kaiten undo* but pull the left foot around and keep the weight behind the right foot. Your left foot should start moving only when the hip turn has already begun, and care should be taken not to lean too far forward or to let the heel of the back foot lose contact with the mat.

⇧ Start from *migihanmi*. Turn the head, hips and feet to the left as in the *kaiten* exercise, but keep your weight on the front foot.

⇧ Step around with the left foot pivoting on the ball of the front foot. Finish in the same posture but facing in the opposite direction.

Shikko - Ground work

Moving on the knees is often difficult to master, but regular practice of *shikko* (knee walking technique) will help to tone the muscles and loosen up the joints. If you persevere and practise *shikko* regularly you will not only notice the improvement in your Aikido also but you will become fitter and much more flexible as well. In Aikido there are no sacrifice techniques as in judo where *tori* deliberately goes to ground to fell an opponent. Whenever an *aikidoka* goes to ground owing to a fall they will immediately attempt to get back up onto the knees to *keiza* posture and from there return to a standing position. However, because it is not always possible to return to a standing position, we learn how to move effectively on the knees with a good Aikido posture.

2 ⟲ Rotate your hips to the left, swinging your feet to the right and lifting your right knee off the mat.

1

⇦ To perform a basic *mai shikko*, start in *keiza* position, sitting on your toes.

3

⇨ Shift the weight in behind the right knee as you place the knee down. Keep your feet together.

4 ⇨ Repeat on the left side.

Points to remember

Because regular repeated practice of technique with a partner makes up the larger portion of Aikido training, it is important that the basics — a mobile posture, straight back, and relaxed, flexible movement with good breath power — are developed properly right from the start. Repeated practice of poor technique will instill bad habits that can be difficult to unlearn later. Progress depends on regular diligent training with a good instructor, but it is also largely dependent on an individual's attitude. If you see your training partner as an enemy to be destroyed then there is very little chance of either of you learning much from the other. That kind of attitude creates fear, hostility and tension, which are not conducive to fluid breathing and movement. *Aikidoka* who are open to the art of Aikido — who relax, enjoy their training and concentrate on the basics rather than being aggressive — make the best students.

ACHIEVING HARMONY

The secret of Aikido is to harmonize ourselves with the movement of the universe and bring ourselves into accord with the universe itself. He who has gained the secret of Aikido has the universe in himself and can say, 'I am the universe. I am never defeated, however fast the enemy may attack. It is not because my technique is faster than that of the enemy. It is not a question of speed. The fight is finished before it is begun.

When an enemy tries to fight with me, the universe itself, he has to break the harmony of the universe. Hence at the moment he has a mind to fight with me, he is already defeated.'

(Memoirs of O Sensei Morihei Ueshiba, from *Aikido* by Kisshomaru Ueshiba — 1966 — Hozansha Publishing Company.)

The principles of harmony

Every attack provides the force (*ki*) required to defend against it. However, it takes training and effort to learn how to connect with the force, harmonize with it, and redirect it into harmless channels.

This is counterintuitive to Westerners, who are accustomed to meeting force with a more powerful force as a means of control. The Eastern concept of Yin and Yang may help to understand the Aikido approach better. Yin and Yang are opposites — negative and positive. Yin is receptive and Yang is creative, and in nature these forces complement one another and create balance. To be in balance it is necessary both to receive and to create. Within Yin there is Yang; within Yang there is Yin. An excess of Yang energy becomes Yin; an excess of Yin gives way to Yang. In Aikido, the lesson of this principle is that an attacker whose attack is excessively hard, fast or over-committed will be put off balance and made vulnerable to counterattack. On the other hand, an attack that is weak or hesitant will be easily overpowered. A good attack is balanced, using properly 'committed' force. This means that you use the weight of your body, tempered by good timing and an alert and receptive posture, not trying to exceed the limits of your own natural flexibility and balance.

Similarly, a defence that is feeble or excessively submissive will be overwhelmed by a powerful attack. The defender will be put off balance and made vulnerable to the follow-up attack. Good defence, and therefore good Aikido, is receptive to the attacking force without being submissive; it is energetic without being excessively forceful. Aikido strives for continuous balance between the attack and the defence. As *tori* in particular, you must work to maintain your own internal calm, balance and alignment and bring *uke* into the centre of your technique to develop control.

Never attempt to block a moving force such as a push, punch or cut by obstructing it. A moving force has momentum, so it requires great force to overcome it. Even if it is successful, the clash may cause injury to one or both parties. It is far more effective to join forces and then lead the force into more positive channels. Blending into an incoming attack means deflecting the attack harmlessly away or leading the attacker into a compromising position where the attacker loses balance or is trapped in a joint lock.

opposite: BREATH POWER THROW

Practise harmonizing with an attack

To prevent injury and to learn proper form it is best to train slowly. Beginners should always train at a slow pace when executing technique, while more experienced *aikidoka* may vary their pace according to the speed of the attack. Training faster is often a substitute for good form, giving a false sense of security because it will work some of the time. Errors in form will be exposed by slower, more powerful attacks and by more experienced attackers working at speed. As a rule, *tori* should move slower than *uke*. The force of the throw is generated not by *tori* but by *uke*'s own attacking force. Once *uke* is off balance, *tori* can apply a projection technique, causing *uke* to fall, or an immobilization technique, causing *uke* to submit. A good attack is well timed, powerful and balanced. An effective defence must overextend or redirect the attacking force to disrupt *uke*'s own balance and guide *uke* into the sphere of *tori*, who then maintains the balance for the remaining movements of both parties.

Grips and strikes are often dealt with using the same technique with subtle variation. The defences described in this chapter are primarily against strikes and punches, but during training they may be taught from grappling attacks, which, although they can be as difficult to deal with as strikes, are less threatening to beginners and allow *uke* to relax and learn to blend with the attack. The illustrations here show strikes because they make it visually easier to illustrate the dynamics of harmonization.

Joint locks

Joint locks employ techniques in which the joints are twisted or overextended until the attacker cannot escape and must give up. In jiu jitsu these would have been breaking techniques where the joints were dislocated or the bones broken. In Aikido, joint locks are used to break balance, direct the attacker, or pin the attacker to the ground in order to force a submission. They are also used as arrest techniques. Tokyo and Hong Kong police are trained to use Aikido joint locks to take an attacker into custody without the use of handcuffs.

Projections and drops

Although in Aikido we talk about 'throws', in fact an *aikidoka* should never physically throw the attacker. Rather, the action is a projection or a drop. Throwing an attacker may be easy enough if the attacker is light but can be extremely difficult against stronger or heavier opponents. O Sensei Morihei Ueshiba was a small man but he used to train with and teach Sumo wrestlers. Despite his five foot stature he could easily project them away by using their own extreme weight and strength against them once their balance had been controlled. This is one of the reasons why women can train with large men in Aikido without a problem if they are sufficiently prepared. O Sensei often used his women students to convince sceptical men of the effectiveness of Aikido. Larger and stronger men are often the ones who struggle most to advance in Aikido because they habitually rely on physical strength. Smaller people have no option but to learn proper form in order to become effective in their technique.

Strikes and cuts

A strike is very similar to the way you hit a nail with a hammer: it focuses the power in order to break through a single weak point. A cut, on the other hand, does not stop when a block is attempted: it slices through or past an obstruction into the target without stopping. In Aikido we teach students to cut and to defend against cuts, because they are more difficult to manage than simple strikes. You will be taught to direct the cut from your body down your arm and through the tips of your fingers. Energy is not concentrated in a single point in your arm or hand but projects along the full extent of the arm and hand blade. If a weapon is used it simply becomes an extension of the arm and hand, giving extra weight and reach.

When it comes to defence you learn to move in towards the attack, using your wrist to control the point of contact, which is usually *uke*'s wrist when you are grabbed or pushed, elbow when *uke* is cutting or punching, or knee when *uke* is kicking. It is vital to control the force of the attack early, so as a rule we enter towards an attack and blend with it while the force and direction from *uke* are strong. Aikido movements are not jerky. During practice, both *uke* and *tori* should strive to maintain an even pace.

The first projection technique shown here, *shomenuchi iriminage*, is a defence against a straight cut to the front of the head, where the force of *uke*'s attack is directed straight at *tori*'s forehead. This is a classic Aikido entry technique, first blending with the force of the attack and focusing on the attacker's centre of gravity in their 'one point' or 'centre'. The first contact is made with the hand blade underneath the attacking elbow, directing the attack past your head to avoid the strike. *Iriminage* or entry technique is used to redirect the attacking force upward and then behind the attacker so that he must fall.

Shomenuchi — straight cut /strike to the forehead required
From the front you can see that the attacker's hands, hips and feet are all in the same line.

⇐ *Uke (at left)* begins to strike, stepping in with the right foot straight toward *tori*. The strike is performed with the fingers spread and the shoulders relaxed.

⇐ Weight is transferred towards *tori* and the *uke*'s arm cuts down, using the hips to drive it.

⇐ *Uke* uses the hand blade (*tekatana*) of his right hand to cut down through *tori*'s forehead. As *uke* strikes, the back foot is brought forward to add weight to the strike.

Shomenuchi iriminage — front strike entry throw

⇨ Start in *hidari migihanmi* position. As *uke* steps forward raising her arm to strike *Tori* enters using *irimiashi* footwork. *Tori's* arms arch upwards, using a cutting action, aiming for *uke's* upper arm close to her elbow.

⬇ Enter behind *uke's* back with the right foot, cutting down with both hands. (Step clear of *uke* and prepare for further attack. *Uke* takes *ushiro ukemi* and turns to face *tori* to repeat the attack on the opposite side.)

↘ When *uke* is off balance, cut upwards with the right hand and turn your hips counterclockwise. *Uke* will have to begin preparing for *ushiro ukemi*.

3 ↘ Begin to turn, using *tenkan* footwork, and leading *uke* around with your right hip. Break *uke*'s balance early by bending your knees and bringing your weight down on her elbow. *Uke* must maintain contact and follow the technique or she will expose her back to *tori*.

↗ Blend your wrist with her strike by rotating the *tekatana* upwards, deflecting the power of the strike without breaking its flow. Push forward with the wrist and elbow as you slide past to the left, allowing the fingers to blend with the attack.

↘ Draw *uke*'s head towards your shoulder using your left hand on the back of the neck close to the head where it is not supported by the strong shoulder muscles. Turn her face away from you by rotating your wrist counterclockwise.

Common mistakes against overhead strikes

⇧ If *tori* attempts to block the cut with the forearm sideways or does not enter strongly he will not be able to maintain posture and will be pushed backwards by *uke*'s power.

⇨ If *tori* attempts to block the cut using the forearm sideways and does not move off the line of attack, the cut will follow through under the block and cut *tori*'s face.

Punches

Punches can take many forms, from karate or kung fu punches through boxing jabs, punches and hooks to street fighting with gouging, elbow strikes and head butts. In Aikido practice, for safety, the attacker is taught never to straighten the elbow, and to keep it down so it cannot be easily locked or broken. The Aikido defence, of course, works even more effectively against attacks which do not adhere to this rule. To teach you to handle unorthodox attacks safely, more senior training will practise against a variety of styles of attack.

Punches to the face are similar to overhead strikes in that they are straight and aim to connect above *tori*'s shoulder height. They are therefore dealt with in much the same way as *shomenuchi* cuts. *Tori* must enter to meet the attack but use body movement to avoid the strike. It is not necessary to move the strike out of the way. *Tori* can enter directly to the side and redirect the attack backwards. This concentrates the power of the technique, but it should still blend with the attack and redirect the balance. *Tori* should breathe out during the projection. *Uke* must be prepared to go down and give way to the technique. Although the technique is not intended to attack the face directly, this may happen with inexperienced *tori* and can be dangerous. Even if the technique is applied gently, the force on the neck can be quite extreme if *uke* resists the redirection.

Many techniques can be executed from a variety of attacks, with only the initial contact being different. For example, if the punch is aimed lower, into the belly, the contact must be performed from the top but the same technique can be used to finish.

Gedantsuki — low punch

⇧ Start in *hidari gyakuhanmi* stance. *Uke* slides forward *tsugiashi* drawing the right hand into a fist aligned with the right hip.

⇧ *Uke* steps forward onto the right foot punching to the belly of *tori*, rotating the hips to power the strike. *Uke* follows through with the punch without overextending or losing balance.

Gedantsuki iriminage — low-punch entry throw

⬇ *Tori* enters to the left with *tsugiashi*, rotating his hips clockwise in time with the punch.

↗ *Uke* (on the right) punches to the belly of *tori* with the right hand.

⇨ *Tori* uses his hand blade to attack upwards to the front of *uke*'s body, blending with the power of the attack.

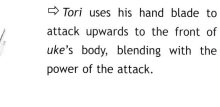

⇦ *Tori* then redirects the *uke*'s upper body and head up and backwards while entering with the right foot.

⬆ *Uke* must take *yoko ukemi* (side protection) to protect his face and neck from injury. (Turn to face *tori* and attack again.)

Direction of attack

Strikes are of two kinds: straight attacks and side attacks. *Tori*'s initial response will depend on the type and the height of the strike. The first priority is to connect safely with the force of the attack. This allows *tori* to feel the balance and tension in the attacker's posture and to work with the force of the attack rather than generate the force themselves. Once *tori* has connected with the attack, it is easier to judge its force and speed and to anticipate changes of direction by the attacker. Using blending techniques, *tori* then extends the attacker out of balance and uses joint locks or projections to neutralize the attack.

Side attacks

Side attacks can be deceptive. *Uke* begins a side strike the same way as a straight one, only rotating the wrist at the last moment to alter the angle of attack. An attack that begins by stepping to the side is more easily covered by a small adjustment of *tori*'s hips and feet and the attacker must cover a greater distance to reach the target, giving *tori* more time to defend. It is easier for a defender to judge the speed of a sideways movement than one that comes straight towards them.

In real situations, of course, the attackers are not bound by any rules and may attack any way they choose. Experienced fighters may be able to attack effectively and at high speed using lateral movements to deceive and to gain a better line of attack. Through repetitive practice, you will learn to use hip rotation and footwork to handle more complex attacks. But the defence against any side attack, whether it is the prescribed *yokomenuchi* attack, a hook punch or even a high roundhouse strike or kick, remains fundamentally the same, especially in the initial stages.

Attacking by moving to the side

If *uke* steps obliquely forward and sideways to attack, *tori* can counteract the attack with a simple hip turn much faster than *uke* can attack.

Yokomenuchi - cut to the side of the head

Uke steps forward with the left foot, raising the right hand as for *shomenuchi*. As *uke* steps forward with the right foot he cuts to *tori*'s face, rotating the wrist, which causes the strike to connect with the left side of *tori*'s head, at the temple.

Shihonage

Yokomenuchi shihonage — cut to the side of the head — four-direction throw

The technique used to harmonize here has its roots in sword technique, hence the sweeping circular movements of arms and hips. *Shihonage* translates as 'four direction throw', meaning that *tori* has the tactical options to project *uke* in any quadrant using this technique. Only one direction is shown here.

⇧ *Uke* starts by attacking *yokomenuchi* with the right hand.

⇧ *Uke* is recommended, at this stage, to take backward *ukemi*.

⇗ ⇘ Cut *uke*'s arm down behind his own feet to completely break his balance. *Uke* should keep his head close to his elbow and wrist to protect his joints from injury.

⇩ As *uke* enters to strike, *tori* also enters on the right foot and cuts down with *shome-nuchi*, blending with the force of the attack.

⇩ *Tori* leads *uke*'s arm down on the left hand side in front of the hips and grasps *uke*'s hand from either side with both hands. Without breaking the flow of *uke*'s *yokomen* cut, *tori* turns his hips clockwise (step sideways with the front foot) drawing the cut to the right to break *uke*'s balance. *Tori* draws *uke*'s left arm down, thus neutralizing a possible secondary attack coming from *uke*'s left side.

⇨ Cut *uke*'s arm upwards and turn his hips toward the back, while stepping through with the left foot.

↘ Continue turning your own hips clockwise until you face towards *uke*'s rear with his wrist in front of your forehead. It is important for *tori* to hold the attacking hand, not the wrist. (Holding the wrist will support it and make the technique less effective.)

Ukemi for shihonage

In *shihonage*, *uke*'s head is thrown to the mat, while the shoulder, elbow and wrist are all being locked. The technique can 'come on' quite suddenly and you need to be prepared to roll. *Uke* may even find it necessary to slap the mat to assist in breaking the fall, as this is one of the more difficult forms of *ukemi* in the early stages. Concentrate on keeping up with the throw. Only roll when *tori* has completely broken your balance and you cannot avoid falling. Rolling too soon can be dangerous as *tori* may be driving your arm in an awkward direction. Keep your head close to your elbow and wrist to protect your joints from injury and concentrate on rolling, using your hips rather than your shoulders. Remember that your role as *uke* is to provide the appropriate attack and then to protect yourself from injury so that *tori* can apply the throw vigorously.

Change your perspective using *kotegaeshi*

Tactically, *shihonage* is useful because it allows *tori* to throw the attacker in any direction, using him as a shield against other attackers. *Kotegaeshi* or 'small wrist turn throw' also allows *tori* to change perspective during the attack to check the rear in case of secondary attackers. Effective against attacks using small weapons such as knives or handguns, *kotegaeshi* is also useful against empty-handed technique, where a relatively small application to the wrist joint results in spectacular falls. As in all projection techniques, *kotegaeshi* uses the force of the attack and overextends it to draw the attacker off balance. This is combined with a wrist lock that threatens to break the attacker's wrist, forcing him to fall in order to protect himself. Although the wrist lock is extremely effective on its own, more advanced practice relies less on this and more on breaking *uke*'s balance and controlling their movement and posture from the moment of contact or even earlier.

In the case of a high punch to the face, *kotegaeshi* is used to change perspective by turning in next to the attacker and using the wrist turn to project the attacker into the path of a second attacker approaching from the rear. Although multiple attack training is for advanced students, developing awareness of the possibility of secondary attack should always play a part in your daily training. You are expected to develop *zanshin*, which means awareness of and connection with everything around you.

Zanshin

Aikido teaches constant preparedness. Even when you believe no threat exists you need to be aware of secondary factors such as restricted spaces, uneven surfaces, obstacles or moving objects that may have to be taken into account if you need to move to defend yourself. *Kotegaeshi* is a good example of this kind of awareness, as *tori* can scan a full 360 degrees of the surroundings while performing the initial entry. This allows *tori* to decide in which direction to throw the attacker and whether or not they can risk taking *uke* down into a pin on the ground.

In the pictures, *tori* is using a projection technique because a potential second attacker would prevent a ground pin against the initial attacker. During the turn, *tori* bends the knees to bring the attacking hand down and does not allow the attacker to come up again where he could regain balance. Note how *tori* keeps his own back straight and head up so he maintains the advantages of relaxed good posture and unobstructed vision. *Uke* strives to regain control by turning around *tori* and attempting to keep the feet under the body, which provides a platform from which to continue the attack and a better position from which to protect the wrist when the technique is applied. When working with beginners, the lock will be applied more slowly and less painfully, allowing the beginner to fall backwards, which is easier to start off with. As *uke*, you practise attacking appropriately and defending your body from injury, while allowing *tori* to apply the technique as vigorously as you can handle so that you learn to fall at any speed even when you are not properly prepared for it.

Jodantsuki kotegaeshi nage — high-punch wrist turn projection

⇩ Start in *hidari gyakuhanmi* stance. As *uke* punches to the face of *tori* using the right hand, *tori* enters to the left with *tsugiashi*, rotating the hips clockwise in time with the punch and controlling *uke*'s elbow with the hand blade.

↻ *Tori* turns, using *tenkan* footwork and extending *uke*'s punch forward and down, breaking *uke*'s balance as he turns. *Uke* keeps the attacking arm extended as protection against *tori*'s counter strike and turns around ready to take advantage of an attacking opportunity.

⇨ *Tori* slides the left hand down onto the attacking hand to take the grip for *kotegaeshi*.

↖ *Tori*, seeing the second attacker, drops the left elbow and steps in behind *uke* to begin the backwards projection. (*Tori*'s right hand is placed against the back of *uke*'s fingers, which are then extended over and down to the mat, causing *uke* to leap over his own wrist to prevent injury. Less experienced *uke*'s may prefer to use *ushiro ukemi*.)

NEUTRALIZING THE ATTACK

In Aikido we harmonize with the attack in order to neutralize it. Projection technique is dynamic and flowing and, because the attacker is released, it has no end or beginning, like breathing in and out. *Uke* attacks. *Tori* avoids the attack, harmonizes with it, neutralizes the danger by good positioning, and projects *uke* away. Using *ukemi* training to receive the projection, *uke* rolls, and rises to attack again. Meanwhile, *tori* has adjusted position and is prepared to receive the new attack and neutralize it once more.

In the *dojo* there is a soft mat, and care is taken to reduce the risk of injury, but in real life it takes judgement to know just how much force is needed to counter a perceived threat. The beginner who has not yet learned restraint will have to use more force than an experienced *aikidoka*. After just one class the beginner will already have learned some basic skills for surviving an attack, but it will take years of training to reach the ideal of *gentle* control, especially when faced with skilled and determined attackers. The more control you have over yourself and the entire situation the less severe the technique you require to stay safe.

Omote and Ura

There are two basic variations to most Aikido forms: *omote*, to *uke*'s front, usually with an entry movement (*irimi*), and *ura*, behind *uke*'s back, which is characterized by turning or *tenkan* movements. In formal training and during grading, *uke* usually performs two *omote* techniques - one on the left and one on the right. This is followed by two *ura* techniques, one from each side. In normal training, *uke* and *tori* swap roles after each set of four techniques, to ensure that everybody has an equal opportunity to perform attack, defence and *ukemi*.

Techniques of immobilization

Although bodies all function mechanically in similar fashion, no two are exactly the same. Different shapes, sizes, strengths and degrees of flexibility present an infinite number of possibilities. And, of course, what the body does is controlled by thoughts and emotions, so individual reactions are not always predictable. The Aikido techniques are designed to help us understand the attacker's body and mind and the nature of the *ki* energy that controls them.

The principles of neutralization are illustrated by techniques of immobilization. These are relatively simple locking and pinning techniques, which are easy enough forms to learn, but take time to perfect. Several of the projection techniques (for example, *shihonage* and *kotegaeshi*, from the previous chapter) also have immobilization variations, which can be applied after the initial projection. The standard Aikido pinning techniques are simply numbered in Japanese from one to six. Only the first three forms are illustrated here.

The first formal pin (*ikkyo*) is a shoulder and arm lock, whereas the second (*nikyo*) and third (*sankyo*) lock the wrist as well. The fourth pin (*yonkyo*) is directs pressure into the muscles and nerves in the wrist. The fifth (*gokyo*, a wrist lock) and the sixth (*rokyo*, an elbow lock) are for use against knife attacks.

Training for immobilization techniques

Locking techniques put pressure on the joints to force a submission, but if applied too quickly or with excessive force they can cause injury. You should bear in mind when training that your partner is not really trying to harm you. If you find you need to apply significant force to *uke*'s arm then you are probably doing

opposite: KAITENNAGE — THE WHEEL THROW

something wrong. If you continue to apply pressure you may injure your partner. You will soon find that nobody wants to train with you and when they do they will resist the technique before you even apply it to protect themselves from injury.

Be patient. Immobilization techniques require several months of rehearsal before you can speed up. In time you also get to know when to ease off and when to firm up on an attacker. You learn this by slowly increasing the pressure of the immobilization until *uke* taps with the hand on the mat to indicate the joint is immobilized. *Uke* will allow the lock to be applied up to the point where further extension will cause damage to the joint, and then tap out clearly to indicate submission. This obviously requires *uke* to trust that *tori* will not apply the lock so quickly so that the joint is injured or continue application after the tap. Apply the lock firmly but slowly, keeping good balance so you can stop promptly when *uke* taps out. Train with as many different partners as you can, because everyone experiences the lock differently. You need to learn what it feels like to be immobilized, so that you can judge for yourself how hard to apply it if you ever have to use the technique out on the street.

Ikkyo — first immobilization technique

The *ikkyo* pin is often referred to as the first principle of Aikido because it encapsulates in classic style the way *tori* meets a direct force with an indirect one and redirects the force so as to immobilize the attacker. In the basic form, *tori* uses the outer hand to control the wrist while the inner hand controls the bend in *uke*'s elbow. *Uke*'s arm is guided in an arc down into the ground, effectively pinning the shoulder into the ground with *tori*'s body weight.

Aihanmi katatedori ikkyo — first pin from single hand gripped across body

⇩ Both *uke* and *tori* face one another with right feet forward and *uke* begins by gripping *tori*'s right wrist with his right hand.

⇩ As *uke* reaches out to attack, *tori* rotates his right thumb down so that the attack makes contact with the back of *tori*'s wrist.

⇩ As contact is made, *tori* rotates the right hand palm upward, which weakens the attacker's grip and allows *tori* to bend *uke*'s arm using the left hand (thumb down) in the crook of *uke*'s elbow. From this position the technique can proceed with either the *omote* or the *ura* form.

Omote (also *irimi* or entry form)

↰ In the *omote* form, *tori* must step forward into *uke*'s space with his right foot slightly to the front of *uke*. *Uke*'s shoulder is rotated forwards using the left hand, while the right hand cuts *uke*'s arm down in an arc towards the third point. (The third point is to the side, midway between *uke*'s feet. It is the point at which an imaginary third leg would be positioned to form a tripod.)

↰ Two more steps, one to the left and one to the right, complete the take-down as the arm is guided down onto the mat.

⇩ *Tori* rotates *uke*'s shoulder into the mat and presses forward and down with his *tekatana* at *uke*'s wrist and elbow. *Tori* keeps pushing *uke*'s arm forward until he taps in submission.

Ura (also *tenkan* or turning form)

⇨ In the *ura* form, *tori* turns away from the attack, allowing *uke* to fall in a downward spiral at *tori*'s feet. To perform this version, *uke*'s arm is cut down as *tori* performs a *tenkan* action, keeping the attacking arm in front of *tori*'s 'one point' while spiralling downward into the mat.

Ikkyo pin

⇩ Once *uke* is on the mat, *tori* kneels down next to him, tucking the left knee into *uke*'s ribs below the armpit, and pushes *uke*'s arm forwards 90 degrees from *uke*'s side.

↰ *Tori* guides *uke* down at his own feet where he can complete the technique with an immobilization.

Gyakuhanmi katatedori ikkyo — first pin from side grip to the wrist

1 ⇧ ⬈ From a side attack *tori* must step across the front of *uke* while *uke* is still approaching and strike to the face with the right hand. This striking technique is called *atemi* and is intended to upset *uke*'s balance and distract his attention. Bring the right foot in behind the left to switch to right posture.

5 ⇦ ⬇ ⬃ *Tori* completes the control with *tenkan* and immobilizes *uke* as before.

2 ⇧ *Tori* draws down *uke*'s arm with his right hand and takes hold of the back of *uke*'s hand. The left hand slides in underneath *uke*'s elbow in preparation for bending the arm.

3 ⬈ ⇨ ⬊ For *omote*, *tori* can enter as for the *omote* version of *aihanmi katatedori ikkyo*.

4 ⇩ For the *ura* version, *uke* should first be drawn to the left and down.

Shomenuchi ikkyo — first pin from strike to the head

⇩ *Shomenuchi ikkyo* is a true test of ability. Although the basic projection and pinning technique is the same as in the previous two forms, the initial contact is very different. As *uke* steps forward to cut to *tori*'s head, *tori* must enter early, directing the force of *uke*'s hand over *tori*'s own head, and...

↗ ... turning the attack by entering *omote* on the right foot.

⇒ Tori enters to the right controlling uke's striking elbow ...

↖ ... and turns *tenkan*, pivoting around the right foot.

Poor timing or a poor angle of entry will result in a painful clash in which the larger, more powerful force will hold sway. With good timing, *uke* will be turned back on himself and pinned in one clean cut on the *omote* side, while the *ura* form will result in *uke* flying around and into the mat when the technique is performed at speed. This technique is difficult to learn without direct instruction from your teacher as there are many small details that can make or break it.

⇐ *Tori* pins *uke's* shoulder to the mat.

Nikyo — second immobilization technique

Nikyo omote is essentially the same as *ikkyo omote* with the addition of a potentially painful wrist lock. The *nikyo* lock is usually performed with the *uke*'s wrist and elbow bent and the forearm parallel to the ground. *Tori* reaches across the body to grip the back of *uke*'s hand with both thumbs pointing in the same direction. The free hand is used to control *uke*'s elbow to stop it from rising as *uke* attempts to escape the lock. For *nikyo ura* there is an extra stage in the technique in which the *uke* is controlled down onto the knees using the wrist lock before the technique is completed with *tenkan* and the pin. The pin for *nikyo* is done with the arm up in the air, which gives *tori* more control to restrict *uke*'s movement.

Katatedori Nikyo (omote)

1 ⤴ ⇦ Starting as per the *ikkyo* version, *tori* uses *atemi* to stop the attack and disrupt balance *tori* moves backwards away from *uke*'s free hand breaking *uke*'s balance forwards grasping the back of *uke*'s hand.

2 ⤴ ⤵ Stepping in to the front of *uke*, *tori* frees her left hand to control *uke*'s elbow upwards from underneath.

⤵ Tori enters as for *ikkyo* to complete the take down twisting *uke*'s palm up and then forward for the pin.

3

Gyakuhanmi katatedori nikyo (tenkan) — second pin from side grip to the wrist (turning form)

1 ⟋ ⇩ ⟍ As *uke* grabs *tori*'s wrist, *tori* steps forward using *atemi* and switches to right posture as for *ikkyo*. Sliding the right hand down onto the back of the hand, *tori* takes *nikyo* grip.

2 ⇨ Stepping forwards with the left foot, *tori* changes back to left posture facing *uke* from the left side.

5 ⇩ The pin is performed by drawing the *uke*'s arm across into the crook of your own left arm, directing the arm downward towards the head, using the body weight.

3 ⟍ Controlling *uke*'s elbow with the thumb underneath and the fingers on top, *tori* draws *uke*'s hand in against the shoulder and bends forward from the waist, applying pressure across *uke*'s wrist and forcing *uke* to her knees.

4

⇦ ⇦ Without releasing the pressure on the joint, *tori* cuts down and performs *tenkan* as for *ikkyo ura*.

Aihanmi katatedori nikyo (irimi) — second pin from crossed hand grip to the wrist (entry form)

1 ⇩↘ As *uke* grabs *tori*'s wrist on the left ...

⇩*tori* traps *uke*'s fingers using the right hand.

2

3

⇨ The fingers of *tori*'s left hand slide over *uke*'s wrist and curl around the wrist, exerting pressure on it. Do not force *uke* down but try to direct the power of *uke*'s fingers back over her own wrist.

6

↘ The pin is performed as in *nikyo ura*.

4

↘ Bend forward from the waist, applying pressure against *uke*'s wrist and forcing her to her knees.

5

↘ Without releasing the pressure on the joint, cut down and enter to the third point as for *ikkyo omote*.

Sankyo — third immobilization technique

While *nikyo* is performed with the wrist and forearm parallel with the ground, *sankyo* locks the wrist with the hand and forearm vertical. While *nikyo* applies pressure across the joint, *sankyo* twists the wrist joint, rotating anticlockwise, with *uke*'s fingers pointing downwards for *sankyo*. *Sankyo* is extremely powerful and can be executed with only one hand, but it is highly recommended that you always use two to be certain of control.

Gyakuhanmi katatedori sankyo (omote)
Starting from *gyakuhanmi katatedori* grip, *tori* begins with *atemi*, changing posture as for *ikkyo*.

⬧ Taking the *nikyo* grip with the right hand, *tori* enters *omote*, cutting as for *ikkyo omote*.

⬅ Instead of controlling the elbow with the left hand, *tori* slides the left hand under *uke*'s arm and takes hold of *uke*'s fingers. *Tori*'s fingers hold the palm of *uke*'s right hand while the thumb and the palm control the back of the fingers.

⬅ Exerting gentle pressure in a twisting action towards *uke*'s centre, *tori* steps forward, cutting *uke*'s hand and forearm down in an arc to the ground.

④ ↗ ⬇ ⬊ Changing hands, *tori* kneels around *uke*'s right shoulder, pinning it vertically while keeping *uke*'s palm firmly against *tori*'s left shoulder.

This book can give you only a taste of what you will learn by studying with a teacher. There are 12 basic attacks and five basic locks, each of which has *omote* and *ura* forms. This makes 120 forms of locks alone. And there are as many variations on these 120 basic forms as there are *uke*, so it is important to practise with as many different *uke* as possible. Train as slowly as possible and work on improving your form until it becomes second nature. This is especially important with *ikkyo*, which is the foundation of many other techniques.

Katatedori Sankyo (ura)

1 ⬇ ↘ Starting as per the *omote* version.

2 ⇨ *Tori* moves sideways away from *uke*'s free hand breaking uke's balance sideways.

3 ⇨ ↘ Stepping in behind *uke*, *tori* changes to *sankyo* grip.

4 ↗ ↘ Entering and turning behind *uke*'s back to complete the take down and pin.

DEVELOPING SKILLS

P hysical strength and agility vary from one person to another, but both can be significantly developed through physical and mental training. By using relaxed breathing and good timing to make the most of what power they do have, people who are smaller and weaker, or even ill or injured, can nevertheless overcome fast and powerful attackers.

The power of breath

Breathing is one of the purest expressions of Aikido. Breath liberates the energy stored in the body. We breathe without having to think about it, and yet we can control our breathing. We can hold our breath; we can breathe too fast, or too slow. The state of a person's breathing tells you as much about their state of mind as it does about their state of health and physical fitness. In Aikido we maintain calm relaxed breathing because this helps to keep the mind calm and relaxed. But more importantly, we use our breath to enhance the technique.

Combining breathing with technique

Breath power is used in all technique. In general we breathe in while receiving and out while projecting, but this is never forced. Breathing must be natural.

For technique to be performed well it is important to unify the mind and body and this can be best achieved by focusing on breath power. Controlled weight transfer energized by good breathing balances and calms the body and mind. Good upper body alignment, stable hips and balanced body energy moving around a fixed centre create the stability and flexibility required for *tori* to move and receive *uke*'s power. It is no coincidence that *ki* is said to be generated from the body's centre of gravity (in the 'one point'). *Ki* can also be understood as the balance of the body's energy. When we restrict our breath or tense our muscles we create *ki* imbalance in the body, resulting in instability and vulnerability.

Practising breath power techniques will help you understand the true spirit of Aikido. Technique without breath power lacks the rhythm and sensitivity needed to generate power with timing and control.

Kokyunage — breath power throw

This is not so much a specific technique as a set of techniques that focus on using breath power in the throw. Although they look simple (and they are), at the same time they are advanced techniques, because of the delicate timing and degree of relaxation required to do them properly. *Tori* must align the body with the attack at precisely the right moment, follow and blend with it, and take control of the movement without any gripping. This takes several months or even years to achieve with consistent control, although it will be experienced to some degree right from the start. Because there is no gripping by *tori*, the technique cannot be forced.

The various other projections illustrated here will help you to understand the concept, because they also embody the principles of breath power. For example *tenchinage* ('heaven and earth throw') is also executed without any grip by *tori*. Alignment of the upper body with the attack, good timing, hip stability, relaxed shoulders and knees and balanced transfer of weight are essential to make this technique work. Because the technique breaks the balance by directing *uke* down with the 'earth' hand and, at the same time, up with the 'heaven' hand, it is common for the technique to stall in the middle, as these two actions cancel each other out. A better understanding of breath power will allow *tori* to extend in both directions without blocking the flow of the attack.

opposite: PROJECTION

Because the *ukemi* for these techniques usually requires more space than for other techniques, they are often practised in groups of two or more attackers.

It is important when taking *ukemi* that you practise with good *zanshin* (awareness) and quickly come to your feet before the next *uke* is thrown on top of you.

Katate ryotedori (morotedori) kokyunage (Ushironage) — two hands to one hand breath-power technique (backward throw)

1 ⇧ *Uke* attacks *tori*, gripping *tori*'s right wrist strongly with both hands.

2 ⤢⤢ *Tori* breathes in, turning the hips counterclockwise, using *kaiten* turning technique. The right hand is drawn down past the centre, palm upwards leading *uke* and then raised upwards towards the end of the turn.

3 ⇨ Without stopping or holding the breath, *tori* turns the hips back towards *uke*, breathing out and cutting down with the arms and projecting *uke* backwards into *ushiro ukemi*.

5 ⇧ When training faster there is no time to step backwards, so *uke* slides feet first under *tori*'s armpit. *Uke*'s feet slide through to the front as they turn sideways, slapping the mat as *uke* drops onto their side. This *ukemi* is more like *yoko ukemi* than *ushiro ukemi* and should be practised at medium pace before attempting full speed attacks.

4 ⇦ *Uke* also breathes in as he attacks and then out as he takes *ukemi*, practising *kokyuryokyu* (breath power). At a slower pace *uke* can step backwards to take the *ukemi* backwards.

Katate ryotedori (morotedori) kokyunage (Tenkan tsugiashi) — two hand to one hand breath-power technique (turn and glide step)

↘ *Uke* attacks *tori* gripping *tori*'s right wrist strongly with both hands.

1

2 ↘ *Tori* breathes in, while turning the hips counterclockwise using *tenkan* turning technique, blends with the attack, and begins to lead *uke* around, using the right hand palm up at hip level.

→

4

↘ *Uke* may project themselves well clear of the throw when there is plenty of space in which to roll. This allows *uke* to roll cleanly back up onto the feet for another attack. (If space is limited, *uke* may be forced into a tighter roll and need to slap the mat to stop the forward momentum sooner. These rolls should be rehearsed without the throw initially until *uke* is more confident. *Tori* should take care not to throw *uke* into other *uke* who may be rolling nearby. This is also part of *zanshin* training. At times an Aikido mat can become very busy and you may have to direct throws onto very small patches of *tatami* if there are a lot of people training.)

3

↗ As *uke* starts to become overextended and passes next to *tori*, *tori* begins to step forward in the same direction as *uke*, leading with the front foot. Breath is exhaled on this step and the wrist rotates gently to project *uke* off balance into *mai ukemi*.

Katate ryotedori (morotedori) kokyunage (Irimi tenkan) — two hand
to one hand breath power technique (enter and turn variation)

1

2 ⟲ *Tori* breathes in, entering to the
left side using *irimi tenkan* footwork something like a matador
stepping past a charging bull.

⇧ *Uke* attacks *tori*, gripping *tori*'s
right wrist strongly with both hands.

3

⇨ Avoiding the main rush of
the attack *tori* blends with
it, turning in a half circle
using the right hand palm
down at hip level.

5

4

⤴ Breath is exhaled
on this step, and the
wrist rotates gently
palm down behind
uke's back. *Uke* now
takes *ushiro ukemi*.

⇨ As the *uke* starts to become
overextended, arriving off balance
next to *tori*, *tori* turns in behind *uke*
using *tsugi ashi tenkan* footwork,
leading *uke*'s hands up over his head.

**Ryotedori kokyunage (Irimi kaiten) — breath-power throw
with both hands grasped (enter and turn variation)**

⤢ *Uke* attacks by gripping both *tori*'s wrists pushing *tori* backwards.

⬇ *Tori* slides to the right side using *irimi kaiten* footwork, avoiding the main rush of the attack. *Tori* blends the left hand with the push from *uke* and projects under *uke*'s grip with the right hand coming up behind *uke* and propelling him forward with a cartwheeling motion from the shoulders.

↘ *Tori* follows through with breath power and extension, projecting *uke* into *mai ukemi*. This fall can cause problems to beginners as there is a tendency to flip over onto the back, so be alert and pay attention to your fall. *Tori* may step through with the right leg for a stronger finishing posture.

⤢ *Uke* is prevented from turning by the extension down the left arm and up the right arm.

Katatedori sumiotoshi (irimi) — corner drop from a side grip to the wrist — (direct form)

⬅ *Uke* grips *tori*'s right wrist with the left hand and begins to punch with the free hand.

⤴ *Tori* breathes in, sliding to the right using *tsugiashi* footwork. *Tori* blends with the attack and leads *uke*'s right wrist to the third point behind *uke*'s feet, rotating the right hand palm downward and bending the knees.

⮕ As the *uke* loses balance to the rear, *tori* enters behind *uke*'s back and uses the left arm under *uke*'s armpit to keep control of *uke*'s balance.

⮧ Breath is exhaled on this step and the left wrist rotates gently to project *uke* (still off balance) into the corner drop. *Uke*'s balance must be well broken, because this technique ends in a drop rather than a projection.

Shomenuchi aikiotoshi — Aiki drop from an overhead strike

⇩ *Uke* begins by attacking the top of the head, using *shomenuchi* on the right side.

⇩ Bending the knees, *tori* slides in under the strike, turning his back to blend with *uke*'s abdomen. The left leg slides in behind *uke*'s front foot and the left arm reaches up across *uke*'s chest as the strike passes over the shoulders.

⇨ *Tori* straightens up, turning the hips to the rear, breaking *uke*'s balance and allowing him to fall.

⇧ ⬀ ⬀ A more difficult variation consists of a scooping action with the right hand behind the *uke*'s right knee to help break balance by sweeping the foot forward and up. Do not attempt to lift *uke*'s feet or you will end up with *uke*'s weight on top of you, which could be difficult to remove.

Yokomenuchi kokyunage — breath-power throw from an oblique overhead strike

⇨ *Uke* begins by attacking the side of the head, using *yoko-menuchi* on the left side.

⇦ ⇗ Bending the knees, *tori* slides in under the strike, turning with the strike to blend his back with *uke*'s abdomen. Using *irimi tenkan*, *tori* leads the strike around the shoulders, encouraging it to follow through.

⇗ ⇘ *Tori* turns the hips to break *uke*'s balance and encourages him to fall forwards following the strike.

Ryotedori tenshinage (Irimi) — heaven and earth throw with both hands grasped (direct form)

⇩ *Uke* attacks by gripping both *tori*'s wrists and pushing her backwards.

⇧ ⬈ *Tori* breathes in, sliding to her left using *tsugiashi* footwork. *Tori* blends with the attack and leads *uke*'s right wrist to the third point behind his feet, rotating her left (earth) hand palm downward and bending the knees. Simultaneously her right (heaven) hand cuts upward across *uke*'s chest, directing his elbow and head upward.

⇨ As the *uke* loses balance to the rear, *tori* enters behind his back and uses both arms to project him backwards. Breathe out as you enter, rotating both wrists inwards to break free from the grips. Completion of the technique can be either a drop or a projection or a combination of both.

The power of timing

Timing is the ability to take the initiative away from the attacker by moving with him and aligning your power with the attack before it reaches you. Even without using specific technique, moving at the moment *uke* commits himself to the attack will upset the rhythm of the attack, enabling you to avoid it and even to control *uke*'s balance. Moving too late will allow *uke* to crowd you and turn his speed and power against you. Moving too early will allow *uke* to use speed to change the attack and redirect his power. Moving too fast will diminish your ability to harmonize with the attack and will rush you as much as it rushes your attacker. The samurai used timing to control the possible attacks available to an opponent by anticipating and pre-empting the enemy.

Although the art of Aikido can be learned without weapons, training with them makes it easier to learn correct timing. Using weapons changes the timing of technique, because the spacing between *uke* and *tori* alters and the kind of blade or staff they use subtly influences the nature of the confrontation. It improves your judgement of distance, and makes it easier to choose an appropriate technique and to see the consequences of a poor one.

Weapons training in Aikido

The historical relationship between weapons training and Aikido is well documented. Morihei Ueshiba himself was a master with sword, staff and bayonet. These influences are very strong and are often demonstrated in the classes, particularly with techniques such as *kokyunage* and *shihonage* in which the empty-handed technique is a direct derivative of a weapon technique. Many of the older teachers who trained with O Sensei or one of his direct students are skilled sword and staff proponents and teach weapons technique in the *dojo*.

Weapons training is less prevalent today. You will find that one teacher will have more experience than another, and with different weapons, and that teachers' attitudes towards weapons training range from fanatical enthusiasm to deliberate avoidance.

Aikiken (do) — Aikido sword

Aikiken form is influenced by the sword forms of O Sensei and other senior Aikido teachers. It is more flowing and receptive than other sword disciplines such as *kendo*, in keeping with the principles of *aiki* (harmony) and the philosophy of using minimal force.

Paired exercises work with space and timing, controlling the lines of attack between the swordsmen. *Aikiken* is usually practised with a wooden sword called *bokken*, which is a weapon in its own right, as its weight and form make it formidable in trained hands. The key benefits of *bokken* training are improved timing, better appreciation of distance, and ability to control the lines of approach that are open to an attacker.

Bokken training begins with basic cuts and strikes. These are called *suburi*. Once you have practised some of these you may start training with a partner. Initially you may practise *kumitachi*, which are predetermined sets of attacks and defences practised with a partner. Many of these *kumitachi* have been handed down from teacher to teacher from the ancient sword schools. Morihei Ueshiba modified them to fit with the principles and spirit of Aikido, but their basic structure comes from older forms.

Jodori — Techniques with the four-foot staff

Jo technique uses a blunt instrument instead of a blade, which means that it is less obviously lethal. In most countries it is illegal to carry a sword in public, whereas a rake or broom handle may be used to perform *jodori* technique. In some countries you need to get a licence even for wooden weapons, so you should check up on local laws. *Jo* differs from sword in that both ends of the weapon are used. It has a longer reach and can be used to thrust, strike or sweep at an opponent. Practice with *jo* will give you a healthy respect for a stick as a weapon. More senior students will learn to defend against attacks by people armed with swords, staffs, knives and handguns. Weapons training is obviously potentially more dangerous than bare hands training and is usually reserved for senior training, or is very carefully controlled by an instructor.

Partnered sword practice (variation 1)

⇨ *Uke* (on the left) and *tori* (on the right), start in *migi aihanmi* posture with sword tips crossed.

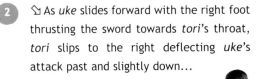

↘ As *uke* slides forward with the right foot thrusting the sword towards *tori*'s throat, *tori* slips to the right deflecting *uke*'s attack past and slightly down...

↘ ...and then thrust to *uke*'s own throat to complete the exercise.

Partnered sword practice (variation 2)

⇩ *Uke* (on the right) and *tori* (on the left), start in *migi aihanmi* posture with sword tips crossed.

⇧ As *uke* steps back with the right foot raising the sword above the head preparing for an overhead cut, *tori* raises the tip of his sword to follow the attackers motion synchronizing his movement with the attacker.

⇦ ...traps *uke's* wrists with his sword.

⇩ *Tori* allows *uke* to raise the sword for a third time but follows the sword up and...

⇩ ...to strike down on top of *uke's* sword.

⬀ As *uke* steps forward cutting downward towards *tori* head, *tori* retreats drawing his sword back down behind his right leg.

⇨ *Uke* raises the sword for a second cut. *Tori* follows the rising sword with his own stepping forward onto the right foot.

⬇ ...changing feet as the sword travels in a circle behind the head and up...

⬆ As *uke* cuts to the head a second time, *tori* steps to the left with the back foot defending the head by raising the sword and...

Partnered sword practice (variation 3); preparing to disarm

1 ↘ *Uke* (on the left) and *tori* (on the right), start in *migi aihanmi* posture with sword tips crossed.

2 ⇐ As *uke* raises the sword above his head preparing for an overhead cut, *tori* raises the tip of his sword to follow the attacker's motion, synchronizing his movement with the attacker and controls *uke*'s wrists with his sword.

3 ↗ *Tori* then slides his hand in between *uke*'s hands and grips the handle of *uke*'s sword.

4 ⇒ *Tori* cuts *uke*'s sword over his hips to throw *uke* and remove his sword.

Tachi dori (Shomen uchi Koshi nage) — disarming a sword attack; hip-throw from a cut to the head

⬇ *Tori* then slides his right hand in between *uke*'s hands...

1

2

3

↗ *tori* raises the left hand blade to follow the attacker's motion, synchronizing his movement with the attacker, and controls *uke*'s wrists.

⬆ As *uke* raises the sword above his head preparing for a cut...

4

⇨ ...and grips the handle of *uke*'s sword from underneath.

7

⇦ *Uke* takes *mai ukemi* and must slap the mat to break the fall.

↘ *Tori* directs the cut started by *uke* over *tori*'s hips...

6

5

↗ ...to throw *uke* and remove his sword.

Tachi dori (Shomen uchi Kokyu nage) — disarming a sword
attack; breath-power throw from a cut to the head

2 ⇗ As *uke* cuts to the head, *tori* steps forward to the left, sliding his right hand in between *uke*'s hands...

3

⇧ As *uke* raises the sword above his head preparing for a cut *tori* raises the right hand blade to follow the attacker's motion synchronising his movement with the attacker...

⇨ ...and grips the handle of *uke*'s sword from the top.

4

6

⇗ *Uke* takes *ushiro ukemi* and must slap the mat to break the fall.

⇨ *Tori* then raises his left arm up the front of *uke*'s face, disrupting *uke*'s balance upwards and backwards and...

5

⇦ ...cutting down to throw *uke* and remove his sword.

Jo dori Nikyo – Staff technique (second pin)

⇧ *Tori* steps slightly to the left turning his hips towards *uke*, leading *uke*'s right hand upwards while disrupting *uke*'s balance.

⇧ *Uke* grabs *jo* attempting to control it from *gyaku hanmi* posture.

⇦ Using his left hand to traps *uke*'s right hand on the *jo*, *tori* cuts the *jo* forward applying *nikyo* pin to bring *uke* down.

⇗ *Tori* then pushes the point of the *jo* under *uke*'s elbow.

⇨ *Tori* leads *uke*'s elbow and shoulder down onto the mat.

⇧ *Uke*'s arm is pinned to the mat using *nikyo* immobilization.

Ken Tai Jo — staff technique; first pin against sword attack

⇨ As *uke* raises the sword above his head preparing for a cut *tori* follows the attacker's motion, synchronizing his movement with the attacker's.

1

2

⇦ As soon as a gap appears *tori* inserts the *jo* between the *uke*'s left arm and his head and enters to the left preventing the strike.

⇩ *Tori* uses *ikkyo* immobilization, also pinning *uke*'s neck to the ground with the *jo*.

5

3

⤢ *Tori* turns his hips towards *uke* as *uke* goes past, leading *uke*'s right hand downwards using the front end of the *jo* while disrupting *uke*'s balance forwards and controlling *uke*'s head with the rear end of the *jo*.

4

⤢ *Tori* then steps forward projecting the *jo* forward and downwards to take *uke* to the mat.

Tachi dori (*Shomen uchi* variation) — disarming a sword attack (from a cut to the head)

1

↗ As *uke* raises the sword above her head preparing for a cut, *tori* raises the right hand blade to follow the attacker's motion, synchronizing his movement with that of the attacker.

2

↗ As *uke* cuts to the head, *tori* steps forward to the left, sliding his left hand in-between *uke*'s hands and grips the handle of *uke*'s sword from the top.

3

⇨ *Tori* then turns his hips towards *uke*, pushing down on the back of the sword blade and raising his left hand up to the front of *uke*'s face...

↘ ...disrupting *uke*'s balance, weakening her grip and cutting to her body with his sword.

4

⇦ *Uke* releases her grip on the sword to escape and...

5

6

⇦ ...takes *ushiro ukemi* to avoid the sword.

Tantodori — defence against knife attack

When working with knife attacks, the hand changes do have to change slightly. *Tori* must be aware where the cutting edge of the knife is facing and will often need to allow a little more space and have better timing in order to successfully defend against such an attack. The techniques explained are two of the easier to perform even though *uchikaiten sankyo* may appear complicated at first.

Tanto tsuki Iriminage — knife thrust (entry throw)

⬀ *Uke* attacks *tori*, stabbing to the stomach with a knife. *Tori* breathes in, entering to the left side using *tsugiashi* footwork to avoid the blade and directing *uke*'s elbow to control the knife thrust.

⬀ As *uke* starts to become overextended, arriving next to *tori*, *tori* continues to disrupt *uke*'s balance by pushing up in front of *uke*'s face and...

⬀ ...breathes out, while stepping through behind *uke* with the right foot, cutting down with the right arm behind *uke*'s back and forcing *uke* into *ushiro ukemi*.
(More advanced students will disarm *uke* during the throw.)

Tanto tsuki uchikaiten sankyo - knife thrust - turn under - third pin

⬃ *Tori* turns the hips clockwise and steps *tenkan* with the right foot to the back leading *uke* into a circle, while griping *uke*'s knife hand from underneath with *tori*'s hand palm up — thumb pointing up *uke*'s arm.

⬀ *Uke* thrusts to *tori*'s stomach with a knife. *Tori* breathes in, entering to the left side using *tsugiashi* footwork to avoid the blade and directing *uke*'s elbow to control the knife thrust.

⬀ *Tori* steps sideways to the left, again leading *uke*'s knife hand down towards his rear to disrupt balance.

8

⇦ ⇦ *Tori* changes hands controlling the knife...

7

⇨ ...and steps *irimitenkan* behind *uke*'s back pushing down on *uke*'s elbow.

9

⇧ ...and pushes against the back of the blade to disarm the attacker.

⇨ *Tori* continues to twist the wrist, leads *uke*'s knife hand down behind *uke*'s own feet...

6

4

⇦ Raising the knife hand, *tori* enters under *uke*'s arm stepping onto the right foot...

5

↘ ...and then turns couterclock-wise, twisting *uke*'s wrist and bringing *uke*'s hand down.

THE WAY FORWARD

Having learned the basics, the new *aikidoka* may want to move on. Some training methods are by their nature more advanced than others. In general, striking techniques are more advanced than grappling ones, but this need not put beginners off. In fact, many beginners are enthusiastic about strikes because they perceive these to be their most significant threat in the street. More difficult to deal with are disorientating attacks such as those from behind or involving repeated strikes, combinations of different kinds of attack, or attacks by multiple assailants.

Advanced training methods
Ushirowaza — attack from the rear

A truly unexpected attack from the rear may be impossible to defend against. However, training in *zanshin* (awareness) will make you more conscious of your surroundings and less susceptible to surprise. You learn this by training on a crowded mat where, to avoid accidents, both *uke* and *tori* must be aware at all times of the other pairs of flying bodies. *Zanshin* is also developed during *randori* (multiple attacker training) in which *tori* must deal with attackers coming from all directions.

Morihei Ueshiba's uncanny ability to anticipate attacks, even from the rear, was one of the main reasons for the awe in which he was held. His *uchedeshi* (live-in training students) were encouraged to try and catch him off-guard at any time. Many attempted to creep up on him, some even at night, when he was apparently asleep. None ever succeeded in surprising him. One story concerns a class he regularly taught to an army unit who were famed for their skills with the bayonet. O Sensei was annoyed when he arrived at the *dojo* to find only one of the officers had arrived for the lesson. After remonstrating with the sole student for his colleagues' rudeness, Morihei stepped out of the *dojo* into the courtyard that led out to the street, where the 'missing' army men leapt at him from all sides with bayonets — only to find that he had disappeared. After a moment of confusion the men turned at a sound from the direction of the street exit. There stood O Sensei, chuckling at them.

In training we do not usually allow an attacker to approach from the rear. We align ourselves so that he must approach from the front or side. To get behind us, he must move very fast. *Uke*'s access to *tori*'s back is restricted by *tori* turning the hips and moving to maintain a safe distance (*ma-ai*). If an attacker comes very fast from one side we may draw him in behind us in order to gain control and to turn him. An attacker who grabs the wrist can be drawn in behind *tori*'s back in order to bring him closer. Once he is close enough that punches and kicks are restricted we can use a lock or projection technique to deal with him.

Jiyuwaza — freestyle training

In *jiyuwaza*, *tori* begins to apply the basic skills to more challenging situations. Both *uke* and *tori* need to have some experience. *Uke* must attack with commitment and may be required to fall in an unexpected or awkward fashion. *Tori* spontaneously selects the most appropriate defence to deal with the attack. *Tori* must use good form (posture, relaxation, breath power, fluid movement and timing) to take the initiative from the attacker and even to limit the possible attacks available to *uke*. Often during advanced training *tori* will not use standard techniques but will adjust and combine techniques depending on the nature of the attack.

opposite: DEFENDING AGAINST MULTIPLE ATTACKERS

GLOSSARY

AI	Harmony	JIYUWAZA	Free-style technique
AIHANMI	Harmonious posture with respect to a partner	JO	Four-foot wooden staff
		JODAN	High
AIKI	Blending or harmonizing with *ki*	JODANTSUKI	Punch aimed at head
AIKIDO	The way of harmony	JODORI	Staff technique
AIKIDOKA	Aikido practitioner	JIU JITSU	Combat art or skills
AIKIKEN	Aikido sword work	KAESHIWAZA	Countertechniques
AIKIOTOSHI	Centre drop	KAITEN	Body rotation
ASHI	Step	KAMAE	Ready position or stance
ATEMI	Defensive strike used to disrupt *ki*	KAMIZA	The focal point in a dojo
BOKKEN	Wooden training sword	KATA	Forms (set patterns of movement)
BUDO	The martial way	KATANA	Samurai sword
DAITORYU AIKI JIU JITSU	Daito School of flexible circular combat techniques	KATATEDORI	Single grip to tori's opposite wrist
DO	'The way of' or 'the art of'	KEIKO GI / GI	Training outfit
DOJO	Place of training	KEIZA	Alternative sitting position on the toes
'DOMOARIGATO GOZAIMASU'	'Thank you very much'	KENDO	The art of sword (Japanese fencing)
DORI	Grab or grip	KI	Vital creative energy, spirit
DOZA	Practice	KIAI	Harmonized, spirited yell
FUNETORI UNDO	Rowing exercise (using breath power)	KIHONWAZA	Basic practice
		KOKYU	Breathing
GEDAN	Low	KOKYUDOZA	Breathing exercises
GEDANTSUKI	Punch aimed below the belt	KOKYUNAGE	Breath-power throw
GOKYO	Fifth pin (wrist lock against knife)	KOKYURYOKU	Breath power
GYAKU	Opposite	KOTEGAESHI	Small wrist turn
GYAKUHANMI	Opposite posture	KUMIJO	Partnered staff technique
HAKAMA	Traditional pants worn by the samurai	KUMITACHI	Partnered sword technique
		KYU	Student grades prior to black belt
HANMI	Basic triangular stance or posture	MA-AI	Safe distance/position
HAPPO UNDO	Eight-direction turning exercise	MAI	Forward
HIDARI	Left	MAI UKEMI	Forward roll
HIDARIHANMI	Left posture	MIGI	Right
HIDARIKAMAE	Left ready position	MIGIHANMI	Right posture
HOMBU	Headquarters dojo (in Japan)	MIGIKAMAE	Right ready position
IADO	The art of drawing the sword	NAGE	Throw, or 'person who is thrown'
IKKYO	The first principle; first pin (arm lock)	NIKYO	Second pin (wrist lock)
		OMOTE	Uke's front
IRIMI	Entry	'ONOGAESHI IMASU'	'Please teach me'
IRIMIASHI	Entry step	O SENSEI	Great Teacher (Morehei Ueshiba)
IRIMINAGE	Entry throw	OTOSHI	Drop

GLOSSARY

REI	Bow	TENKAN (ASHI)	Backward turning step
ROKYO	Sixth pin (elbow lock against knife)	TENCHINAGE	Heaven-and-earth throw
		TORI	The person who is attacked and executes the technique
RANDORI	Defence against multiple attackers		
RANDORIWAZA	Free training	TSUGIASHI	Glide step from front foot
RYOTEDORI	Both wrists grasped	TSUKI	Punch or thrust
RYU	School	UCHI	Strike or cut
SAMURAI	Warrior class of feudal Japan ('One who serves')	UKE	The person who attacks and then receives the technique
SANKYO	Third pin (wrist lock)	UKEMI	Protecting yourself from injury while receiving technique
SEIZA	Traditional sitting position		
SENSEI	Teacher ('The one who goes before')	UNDO	Exercise
		URA	Uke's rear
SHIHONAGE	Four-direction throw	USHIRO	'Backward' also 'from behind'
SHIKKO	Knee walking	USHIRO UKEMI	Backward roll
SHODAN	First degree (black belt)	USHIROWAZA	Attack from the rear
SHOMEN	The forehead	WAZA	Technique
SHOMENUCHI	Cut (or strike) to the forehead	YOKO	(to the) side
SUBURI	Basic sword cuts and strikes repeated for perfection of form	YOKOMENUCHI	Cut to the side of the head
		YOKO UKEMI	Protection when falling sideways
SUMIOTOSHI	Corner drop	YONKYO	Fourth pin (nerve lock)
SUWARIWAZA	Both partners sitting	ZANSHIN	Balanced and aware state, 'connection of spirit'
SUWARIWAZA KOKYUDOZA	Sitting breath power exercise		
		ZAREI	Sitting bow
TACHIDORI	Disarming techniques	ZAZEN	Sitting meditation (from Zen Buddhism)
TACHIREI	Standing bow		
TAISABAKI	Body movements		
TANTO	Wooden training knife		
TATAMI	Traditional Japanese straw mats		
TEGATANA	Hand blade		

ACKNOWLEDGEMENTS

The publishers thank all the models who participated in the sequences depicted in this book, namely: Owen Williams, Anne Allemann, John Ulster, Lana Poolman, David Chaplin, Fazlu Arnold, Richard Kohl, Mark Yeadon, Luke Rawsthorne, Nick Hurley and Jayne Vlok

USEFUL CONTACTS

INTERNATIONAL AIKIDO ORGANIZATIONS

INTERNATIONAL AIKIDO FEDERATION — THE AIKIKAI FOUNDATION
- 17—18 Wakamatsu-cho Shinjuku-ku, 162-0056 Tokyo, Japan
- Tel: + 81-3-3203-9236
- Fax: + 81-3-3204-8145
- E-mail: ueshiba@media.or.jp
- Website: www.aikido-international.org

ARGENTINA
- ASSOCIACION ARGENTINA DE AIKIDO
- Juan de Garay 2244, Olivos-1636, Prov. de Buenos Aires
- Tel: +54-1-791-4518
- Fax: +54-1-791-4518

BRAZIL
- FEDERAÇÃO PAULISTA DE AIKIDO
- Rua Leonardo da Vinci 38, V. Guarani, São Paulo, 04313-000   S.P. CEP
- Tel: +55-11-5017-3803
- Fax: +55-11-578-2803
- E-mail: contato@fepai.org.br
- Website: www.fepai.org.br

CANADA
- CANADIAN AIKIDO FEDERATION
- 56 Somerset Park SW, Calgary, Alberta T2Y 3H4
- Tel: +1-403-201-7108
- E-mail: aikido-caf@the.link.ca
- Website: www.link.ca/aikido-caf/

FRANCE
- FÉDÉRATION FRANÇAISE D'AÏKIDO AÏKIBUDO ET AFFINITAIRES
- 11 Rue Jules Vallès, 75011 Paris
- Tel: +33-1- 4348-2222
- Fax: +33-1-4348-8791
- Website: www.aikido.com.fr
- E-mail: ffaaa@aikido.com.fr

GERMANY
- AIKIKAI DEUTSCHLAND E.V. — FACHVERBAND FÜER AIKIDO IN DEUTSCHLAND
- Steinäcker 19, D-94234 Viechtach
- Tel: +49-9942-7135
- Fax: +49-9942-7136
- E-mail: R.T.Hofmann@t-online.de
- Website: www.aikikai.de

ITALY
- AIKIKAI D'ITALIA
- Casella Postale 4202, 00185 Roma Appio
- Tel: +39-0677-208661
- Fax: +39-0677-208658
- E-mail: aikital@mclink.it
- Website: www.aikikai.it

NEW ZEALAND
- NEW ZEALAND AIKIDO FEDERATION
- P.O. Box 11241, Ellerslie, Auckland
- Tel: + 64-9-379-3777
- E-mail: takase@english.co.nz
- Website: www.geocities.com/Tokyo/Temple/1883/

NORWAY
- NORGES AIKIDOFÖRBUND / NORWEGIAN AIKIDO FEDERATION
- Daas Gate 1, 0259   Oslo
- Tel: +4722557028
- Fax: +4722855269
- E-mail: naf@aikido.no
- Website: www.aikido.no

POLAND
- POLSKA FEDERACJA AIKIDO
- ul. Zakopia_ska 4/3, 45-218 Opole
- Tel: +48-77-457-7868
- E-mail: sekretariat_PFA@wp.pl
- Website: www.aikido.org.pl

PORTUGAL
- FEDERAÇÃO PORTUGUESA DE AIKIDO
- Rua de Coimbra, No. 59, 3o Dto, P-2775 Carcavelos
- Tel: + 351-1-453-5207
- Fax: + 351-1-453-5308

SOUTH AFRICA
- AIKIDO FEDERATION OF SOUTH AFRICA (AFSA)
- P.O. Box 1182, Heidelberg 1438
- Tel: +27 11 744 0009
- Fax: +27 11 744 3568
- E-mail: info@aikido.org.za
- Website: www.aikido.org.za

INTERNATIONAL AIKIDO ORGANIZATIONS

SPAIN
- FEDERACION ESPANOLA DE JUDO Y DEPARTES ASOCIADOS
- Aikido Department, Hortaleza, 108-3 dcha, 28004 Madrid
- Tel: +34 915 416 250
- Fax: +34 915 476 139

SWEDEN
- SVENSKA BUDOFÖRBUNDET AIKIDOSEKTIONEN
- Idrottens hus, 123 87 Farsta, Sweden
- Tel: +46-8-6056000
- E-mail: aikido@budo.se
- Website: www.budo.se/aikido

UNITED KINGDOM
- BRITISH AIKIDO BOARD
- 6 Halkingcroft, Langley Slough Berkshire SL3 7AT.
- Tel: +44-(0)1753 577 878
- Fax: +44-(0)1753 577 331
- Website: www.bab.org.uk

- BRITISH AIKIDO FEDERATION
- Yew Tree Cottage, Toot Baldon, OX44 9NE Oxford, UK
- Tel: +44-(0)1865 343 500
- Fax: +44-(0)1865 343 500
- E-mail: BAF1@btinternet.com
- Website: www.bafonline.org.uk

- IRISH AIKIDO FEDERATION
- 61 Seafield, Wicklow Eire
- Tel: +353-404-67899
- Fax: +353-1-671-8454
- E-mail: aikido@indigo.ie
- Website: indigo.ie/~aikido/

- SCOTTISH AIKIDO FEDERATION
- Woodside Pirn road, Peebles, EH44 6HJ   Innerleithen

- Tel: +44-1698-831451
- Fax: +44-1698-823973
- E-mail: seoras@swhoorders.co.uk

USA
- UNITED STATES AIKIDO FEDERATION
- 142 West 18th Street
- New York, NY 10011
- Tel: 212-242-6246

- AIKIDO SCHOOLS OF UESHIBA
- 29165 Singletary Road
- Myakka City FL 34251

- AIKIDO SHOBUKAN DOJO
- 421 Butternut Street NW
- Washington DC 20012
- Tel: 202-829-4202
- E-mail: info@aikido-shobukan.org
- Website: www.aikido-shobukan.org

- BOULDER AIKIKAI
- 2424 30th Street' Boulder CO 80301
- Tel: 303-444-7721
- Website: www.boulderaikikai.org

INTERNATIONAL YOSHINKAN AIKIDO FEDERATION (IYAF)
- AIKIDO YOSHINKAN HONBU DOJO
- 3F Takayama Building, 2-28-8 Kami-Ochiai' Shinjuku-ku Tokyo 161 Japan
- Tel: 81-3-3368-5556
- Fax: 81-3-3368-5578
- Website: www.yoshinkan.net/-English

KI SOCIETY
- KI NO KENKYUKAI (World Headquarters)
- 3515 O-aza Akabane, Ichikai-machi, Haga-gun Tochigi-ken Japan
- Tel: 01181-0285-68-4000
- Fax: 01181-0285-68-4004
- Email: headquarters@ki-society.or.jp
- Website: www.ki-society.or.jp

- KI AIKIDO USA
- PO Box 75433, Seattle WA 98125-0433
- Tel: 206-527-2151
- Fax: 206-522-8702
- Email: contact@ki-aikido.net
- Website: www.ki-aikido.net

- BRITISH KI SOCIETY
- 5 Hopkins Road, Coundon, Coventry CV6 1BD
- Tel: 02476 598147
- Website: www.ki-society.org.uk
- Email: info@ki-society.org.uk

TOMIKI AIKIDO
- SHODOKAN AIKIDO - TOMIKI
- 1-28-7 Hannan-cho, Abenu-ku, Osaka, 545-0021 Japan
- Tel: +81 (6) 6622 2046
- Email: shodokan@nifty.com
- Website: homepage2.nifty.com/shodokan/en

INDEX